WJEC/Eduqas
Religious Studies
for A Level Year 2 & A2

Philosophy of Religion

Revision Guide

Gregory A. Barker and Peter Cole

Published in 2019 by Illuminate Publishing Ltd, P.O. Box 1160, Cheltenham, Gloucestershire GL50 9RW

Orders: Please visit www.illuminatepublishing.com

or email sales@illuminatepublishing.com

British Library Cataloguing in Publication Data

A catalogue record for this book is available from the British Library

ISBN 978-1-911208-97-6

Printed by Standartų Spaustuvė, Lithuania

3.19

The publisher's policy is to use papers that are natural, renewable and recyclable products made from wood grown in sustainable forests. The logging and manufacturing processes are expected to conform to the environmental regulations of the country of origin.

Every effort has been made to contact copyright holders of material reproduced in this book. If notified, the publishers will be pleased to rectify any errors or omissions at the earliest opportunity.

Editor: Geoff Tuttle

Design and Layout: John Dickinson Graphic Design

Cover design: EMC Design Ltd, Bedford

Cover image: Mellimage

Image credits

p.1 Mellimage; p.6 FGC; p.7 Suchandan Bhowmick; p.8 Friska M; p.12 A.B.G.; p.13 Stuart Miles; p.15 Creative Images; p.18 Ryan DeBerardinis; p.19 Prazis Images; p.21 (bottom) rigsbyphoto; p.21 (top) Rawpixel.com; p.24 DyziO; p.25 Dmitry Naumov; p.26 Cavee; p.30 emc; p.31 Bochachete / Public domain; p.32 Everett Historical; p.36 Crowds of sick people and clergy gathering at the tomb of F. de Paris where people had been cured. Engraving / Wellcome Collection; p.37 Everett Historical; p.38 Motortion Films; p.42 (left) bogdanhoda; p.42 (right) Ross Gordon Henry; p.43 Maria Savenko; p.44 TypoArt BS; p.48 savitskaya iryna; p.49 FXQuadro; p.50 Valery Rybakow; p.51 Nomad_Soul; p.52 Giordana Aita; p.56 Photoraidz; p.57 Roman Samborskyi; p.58 grafvision; p.62 Elnur; p.65 lazyllama; p.68 Evgeny Atamanenko; p.70 Chinnapong; p.74 Budimir Jevtic; p.75 Jacob Lund; p.76 Rad K.

Contents

About Trigger revision

How do I manage all of the information?

We've created these revision guides to help you manage all of the content that you have learned in your A-Level studies and help you apply this to an exam.

Thus, these guides are different from a textbook. Textbooks develop your skills of knowledge and understanding and are supported by evidence and examples. They also equip you with the skills of critical analysis and evaluation in response to the issues relevant to the content so that you can form your own judgements. The Illuminate textbooks also contain ways that you can work with the content to organise and present material in an effective way.

A revision guide, however, prepares you for the final hurdle: transporting everything you have learned into an exam situation.

One of the challenges of this A-Level course has been managing the sheer amount of information from the themes you have studied. A traditional way of doing this is to reduce the material into a condensed block of notes. This can be very useful as a way to summarise the content but may still leave you without a way to manage, remember and also effectively transfer material in an examination situation. This is why we recommend the Trigger concept.

The Trigger concept

A 'Trigger' is simply a way of prompting the 'unpacking' or 'downloading' of the information required for an examination, that is, the basic materials to display your AO1 and AO2 skills.

A Trigger is not always the same as a key term. A Trigger tends to indicate something essential but also points beyond itself for further development. However, some key terms are quite naturally Triggers whilst others are contained within the Triggers.

How does a set of Triggers work?

Our Trigger concept helps with memory stimulation and further development. It is like a reverse cloze exercise – instead of filling in words in a text, the Triggers are presented, and the rest of the text has to be added! The task, then, is to create activities that can help fill the gaps around the missing text by utilising the Triggers you have.

Create your own zip Trigger lists on your mobile devices to help you revise before entering the examination.

Benefits of Triggers

Triggers are:

- Portable (easily transferable to an examination)
- Convenient, practical and readily accessible (something simple enough to transfer to a portable device)
- Concise and efficient (compact and manageable)
- Precise (accurate, focused on the vital elements).

How to use this book

1. Choose a subtheme and read through the Knowledge and understanding area; you will notice that the Triggers are highlighted.
2. Now, go to the AO1 Activity for that subtheme. This asks you to work with a 'zip file' image of the Triggers. You will create your own lists and definitions; sometimes you will be asked to find missing Triggers or to create the 'zip file' for yourself.
3. Read though the Evaluation section. Take note of the Triggers (these are always presented in terms of controversies).
4. You are now ready to take on the AO2 activities for that subtheme, studying the 'zip files' we have presented and creating your own lists, definitions and notes. Sometimes, we will ask you to find missing Triggers or to create the 'zip file' for yourself.
5. At the end of this book you will see examples of Triggers at work in AO1 and AO2 responses. There are also practical insights to help you with your examination.

Key features

In each theme

Specification Links – relevant to the subtheme

AO1 Knowledge and understanding – the most essential aspects of AO1 elements from the specification

AO2 Evaluation and critical analysis – the most essential AO2 material, highlighting three specific controversies for each Specification issue

Triggers – words for AO1 and AO2 highlighted in the main text and then presented in a zip file graphic

Trigger Quotes – easily memorisable short quotations that can be applied to an exam response

Quick Revision – ideas to help you get ready for the exam

Spotlight: evaluative judgements – insights you can use to form a judgement

Trigger activities – these help you to unpack and use the Triggers as a basis for an answer

At the end of the book

Using Triggers to create exam answers – examples of Triggers helping to create a suitable answer

Synoptic Links – examples of how other areas of the Specification can enhance or support answers

AO1 responses: essential guidance

AO2 responses: essential guidance

These sections share insights to help you respond to the WJEC/Eduqas Specification requirements.

We are excited by these books and hope they will help ease the burden and enable you to manage effectively the content involved in the new A Level.

Richard Gray
Dr Greg Barker
Peter Cole

Specification Link

Religion as an illusion and/or a neurosis with reference to collective neurosis; primal horde; Oedipus complex; wish fulfilment and reaction against helplessness. Supportive evidence.

AO1

What is ... Knowledge and understanding ?

This is the skill that involves *selecting* the relevant and appropriate information, *organising* it and then *presenting* it through a *personal explanation* that may involve the use of supporting *evidence* and *examples*.

Freud looked to the subconscious for the explanation of religious belief and practices.

TRIGGER QUOTES

... the ceremony of the totem-feast still survives with but little distortion in the form of Communion. **(S. Freud)**

Theology is anthropology. **(L. Feuerbach)**

Belief in the gods seems to have its roots in human desires and fears, particularly those associated with self-preservation. **(R. Taylor)**

Theme 2D: Sigmund Freud

Freud's explanation of religious belief

- ▢ A **psychological approach** to religion seeks to explain human behaviour and religious beliefs without referencing the idea of a God.
- ▢ Sigmund Freud was the founder of psychoanalysis, which focused on investigating the role of **the unconscious mind**.
- ▢ He saw a connection between the display of **neurotic behaviour**, such as compulsive repeated action (e.g. repeatedly checking if door closed), and the behaviour of some religious people (repeating of confession).
- ▢ What explained this behaviour was the **repression of impulses** that were viewed as temptations one 'ought not' to have. This, in turn, led to a sense of guilt.
- ▢ So, for instance, the religious ritual of prayer becomes an unconscious protective measure to overcome and **displace** this sense of guilt.
- ▢ He claimed that these religious rituals are found **universally** and so concluded that there must be a collective neurosis originating from traumas deep within the psyche.
- ▢ Indeed, Freud looked to **collective neurosis** and other theories as the explanation for all forms of neurosis.
- ▢ Influenced by the writings of **Charles Darwin**, Freud identified the source of these universal guilt feelings in his primal horde theory.
- ▢ This theory argued that the father, as an **alpha male**, possessed all of the child-bearing women in the horde. Over generations in the **primal horde**, the sons killed their father in order to possess the women and this led to guilt.
- ▢ This guilt was later displaced by the creation of animal **totems** (representing the father), which became symbols of the tribe. Over time, the totem was worshipped.
- ▢ Freud regarded the **sexual impulse** as the most basic impulse and at the source of most psychological problems.
- ▢ Freud found another explanation of neurosis, the '**Oedipus complex**'. Oedipus was a prince in Greek mythology who unwittingly killed his father and married his mother. This type of neurosis resulted when sexual feelings of boys towards their mother and resentment towards their father are repressed.
- ▢ The **repressed guilt** is again displaced through neurotic behaviour exhibited through, among other things, the beliefs and practices of religion.
- ▢ For Freud, religion was an illusion that stemmed from our **wish fulfilmen**t – our deepest longings and desires, such as justice and to escape death.
- ▢ He also saw religion as stemming from our lack of security and our reaction against **helplessness** when confronted by natural forces.
- ▢ Freud based support for his Oedipus complex theories about religious belief from his psychoanalysis of patients suffering from **neurosis**.
- ▢ **Case studies** showed him that repressed sexual feelings were at the root of the neurosis.

- His view of the **interpretation of dreams** further supported the role of repressed memories and guilt. He argued that religion stemmed from these guilt complexes.
- **Modern research** indicates that unconscious conflicts contribute to anxiety symptoms.
- Freud viewed evolutionary theory as supportive of his views that the **sex drive** was the key to understanding human behaviour, especially guilt.

Challenges

- The primal horde was mere **speculation** by Darwin. Though the primal horde had been observed among apes, there is no evidence it has been part of any human culture.
- Freud took the theory **out of context** and exaggerated it.
- Even Freud admitted that the primal horde had **never been observed** amongst human beings.
- There is a **lack of evidence** for primal crime from totems and totem meals.
- Freud was influenced by the **discredited** Lamarckian theory of inheritance of acquired characteristics.
- **Anthropologists** have shown a wide variety of religious beliefs, which counts against a universal Oedipus complex explanation for religious belief.
- A study of the **Trobriand culture** suggested that sex has nothing to do with religion. In their culture, though they had a religion, they had a different family structure and there was no evidence of the Oedipus complex.
- God as father is **not the only image** of God in many religious traditions. Freud was too focused on Judaism and Christianity.
- He **ignored** religions that had female deities or had no god at all.
- Freud based his Oedipus complex theory on only five main cases and then **generalised**.
- Freud's theories are **non-scientific** since they cannot be falsified. They are compatible with all possible observations.
- Freud's 'data' from psychoanalysis can be questioned because of the problem of **suggestibility** that can distort findings involving clinical evidence.
- **Recent events** uncovering child sexual abuse in the home may suggest that many of the childhood claims of seduction that Freud dismissed as childhood fantasies, were actually genuine sexual traumas in the home.

Freud explained male gods but gave little account of why some cultures had goddesses.

TIP

Spot the Triggers!
The words in blue are Triggers — key words and phrases that can help you remember knowledge and understanding in this area.

Specification Link

Challenges to Freud's theories about religious belief, including lack of anthropological evidence and no firm evidence for universal Oedipus complex. Evidence basis too narrow.

❝TRIGGER QUOTES❞

Freud did not refer to the most normal populations when evaluating the validity of religion, but instead inferred from a minority population of his already-sick patients.
(F. Westendorp)

Freud, of all people, should have been able to recognise his unconscious desires to potentially destroy religion in order to ... pay back on a traumatic religious experience he had in his childhood. **(G. Zilboorg)**

Freud erects the messiahship of science without observing that scientism is, itself, a faith of illusion. **(B. Flatt)**

Quick Revision

Write down the three main theories that Freud developed that he claimed accounted for religious belief. In your own words, describe: (i) what evidence did he offer to support each theory and (ii) what is the main challenge against each theory. Explain which theory you think is the strongest and give your reasons. This will help you with an exam question in this area.

What is ... Evaluation and critical analysis **?**

The AO2 skills of evaluation and critical analysis mean engaging with the controversies surrounding a subject. This is more than merely describing or listing the points made about a controversy. To achieve this, one weighs up strengths and weaknesses of various sides and takes a position. On the right are three controversies for each issue – you can engage in these by extending their arguments (adding examples, quotes or other details), weighing up their strengths and weaknesses, and coming to a conclusion.

OCD
Obsessive Compulsive Disorder

Is the ritualistic behaviour in religion parallel with obsessive behaviour displayed in neurosis, and do they stem from the same cause – repressed memories?

❝ TRIGGER QUOTES ❞

In the long run nothing can withstand reason and experience and the contradiction which religion offers to both is all too palpable. **(S. Freud)**

Freud's belief that there is no God is an equally infantile (Oedipal) wish fulfilment superimposed on adolescent rebellion against authority. **(M. Westphal)**

Issue:
How far can religious belief be considered a neurosis?

Three evaluative controversies!

□ **Controversy 1:** *Are rituals in religion the same as obsessive behaviour in neurosis?*

There certainly does seem to be **some similarity** between compulsive repeated actions that are related to obsessional neurosis and repeated patterns of religious rituals that religious people perform. They feel uneasy if they neglect the actions and they are meticulous about the way they perform them. However, although Freud argued that both types of actions were caused by repressed instinctual impulses, how compelling is the evidence? For obsessional neurosis, it seems based on very **few case studies** and on theories that **cannot be falsified**. In contrast, religious belief and practice originates from actual events and teachings by religious founders rather than repeated actions.

□ **Controversy 2:** *Does the Oedipus complex explain the belief in God as father?*

It is generally recognised that the **sex drive** is a strong basic instinct. According to Freud, the Oedipus complex, if unresolved, leads to neurotic behaviour. This childhood guilt about the father explains why God is always described in terms of a father figure. It cannot be denied that religious thinking is very **male-centred**. However, Freud seems to jump from explaining neurotic behaviour in his patients by the Oedipus complex to using the same theory to explain religion. **Cultures are so varied** involving family structure and religious practices that it is hard to see how the Oedipus complex can be universal or the cause of religion.

□ **Controversy 3:** *Is Darwinism a valid source for the theories of psychoanalysis?*

Freud claimed that Darwinian biology and its theories were foundational to psychoanalysis. The survival genes included a high sexual drive to facilitate survival. Hence, Freud viewed the **sex drive as central** to any account of human behaviour. However, to demonstrate that is difficult since it is **unfalsifiable**. Whatever the neurosis, it can always be claimed it is because of some repression or other. Freud appealed to the primal horde and the Lamarckian theory to account for the transmission of guilt – but **both are discredited**.

Sp🔘tlight: **Evaluative judgements**

This section contains a special insight that you can use to form a judgement.

If religion is a form of neurosis, then what is the cause? Is it the primal horde theory or the Oedipus complex theory? Freud seems to contradict himself by having both theories. If these are universal causes, how can you tell which of the two it is? The whole business of identifying causes from within the subconscious must be speculation and cannot be empirically tested.

Issue:

How adequate is Freud's explanation of religious belief?

■ **Controversy 1: *Was Freud right about the role of* the unconscious?**
Very few today would argue against the idea of the unconscious mind and would accept the **central role** it plays in human actions. Although the unconscious mind exists, it may not exist or function in the way that Freud suggested. The idea of the ego, id and superego is now rejected, but modern science does still hold to the view that the brain can be compartmentalised. Many cognitive scientists such as **Daniel Dennett** would argue for multiple models of consciousness working in parallel. Freudian psychotherapy is still practised but other therapies, such as **behavioural therapy**, are also effective, though its methodology is diametrically opposed to Freudianism.

■ **Controversy 2: *How scientific was Freud in his approach?***
Certainly, Freud regarded himself as a scientist and saw psychoanalysis as **a new science**. He claimed his theories were based on an incalculable number of observations and experiences. However, what is the characteristic of something scientific? According to **Karl Popper** it is that a scientific theory must be at least falsifiable in principle. Critics, such as Adolf Grunbaum, claim that Freud's theories are compatible with every state of affairs and so cannot be falsified. Therefore, they are not scientific. They **evaded** any empirical test. In addition, Freud was **inclined to ignore** information that was contrary to his theories rather than attempting to account for any variants or anomalies.

■ **Controversy 3: *Did Freud understand religion?***
For Freud, **theology was anthropology**. It was all about the study of human behaviour and societies in the past and present. He held a **negative view** of religion in that he saw it as a neurosis that needed to be treated; an illusion derived from a mix of repressed thoughts, guilt and wish fulfilments. Religion, for Freud, consisted of sacred acts and rituals. However, for many people religion can be about mysticism or about a set of beliefs and doctrines that is supported by evidence. Freud showed a certain **naivety and ignorance** towards religion. He **dismissed** the reading of books about religion on the grounds he already knew the results. This ignores the maturity and complexity of religious traditions. It is certainly not clear that he really understood the essence of religion.

Sp⚙tlight: Evaluative judgements
This section contains a special insight that you can use to form a judgement.

Is Freud correct in focusing on the 'father figure' as the central feature of religion? Certainly, some religions are very patriarchal but Freud only drew from Christianity and Judaism as his examples of religion. He ignored religions such as Hinduism with its female deities and Buddhism, which arguably has no god. There are important expressions of religious belief that do not centre on God as father.

TIP

Do not use a Trigger quote in an exam response that just repeats what you have said in your answer. It should add something so that you can explain how it fits into your argument and develops it.

Quick Revision

Make a list of three examples of obsessive behaviour and then three examples of religious behaviour that Freud regarded as similar to obsessive behaviour. In your own words, explain (i) how they could be seen as similar and (ii) how they could be seen as different. How convincing do you find Freud's argument about their similarity? Give your reasons. This will help you with an exam question in this area.

AO1 Trigger revision activity

A ZIP

Freud's explanation of religious belief

a psychological approach

the unconscious mind

neurotic behaviour

repression of impulses

displace

universally

collective neurosis

Charles Darwin

alpha male

primal horde

totems

sexual impulse

Oedipus complex

repressed guilt

wish fulfilment

helplessness

neurosis

case studies

interpretation of dreams

modern research

sex drive

1 Here is your zip file of portable Triggers. **2** Practise 'downloading' your zip file of Triggers from memory. See how many you can recall on first attempt. **3** When you are confident enough, order the Triggers into a list as you may do in an examination situation.

Why Trigger? Remember, your Triggers are to help you transfer your knowledge and understanding in a manageable, efficient and portable manner.

 TIP

5 Now read through your descriptions and think about ways in which you could develop these using your Trigger quotes. **4** Attempt to write one clear sentence to define each Trigger.

B ZIP

Challenges

discredited

never been observed

speculation

recent events

suggestibility

not the only image

generalised

ignored

out of context

1 Fix the zip file! There are four Triggers missing from this zip file – find them and add them in. **2** There's another problem: the Triggers are out of order! Put them in the same order as they appear in the AO1 section above. **3** Practise 'downloading' your zip file of Triggers from memory. See how many you can recall on first attempt.

6 Now read through your definitions and think about ways in which you could develop these using your Trigger quotes. **5** Attempt to write one clear sentence to define each Trigger. **4** When you are confident enough, order the Triggers into a list as you may do in an examination situation.

AO2 Trigger revision activity

A **ZIP**

Is religious belief a neurosis?

obsessive behaviour	God as father	Darwinism
Some similarity, few cases, cannot be falsified	Sex drive, male-centred, cultures are so varied	Sex drive as central, unfalsifiable, both are discredited

 1 Here is your zip file of portable Triggers.

2 Practise 'downloading' your zip file of Triggers from memory. See how many you can recall on first attempt.

 3 When you are confident enough, order the Triggers into a list as you may do in an examination situation.

5 Now read through all your sentences and think about ways in which you could develop these using your Trigger quotes, further examples, and noting strengths and weaknesses.

 4 'Double-click' each Trigger in your memory – what can you say about an evaluative point of view in a clear sentence? Write this down. Do this for each Trigger in turn.

REVISION TIP

Using Trigger quotes
When you choose the Trigger quotes that you wish to use make sure that you explain how they are relevant.

B **ZIP**

Is Freud's explanation of religious belief convincing?

Naivety and ignorance, theology was anthropology, dismissed, negative view	evaded, inclined to ignore, a new science	Daniel Dennett, the unconscious

1 Fix the zip file! There are three Triggers missing from this zip file – find them and add them in.

2 There's another problem: the Triggers are out of order! Put them in the same order as they appear in the AO2 section above.

3 Practise 'downloading' your zip file of Triggers from memory. See how many you can recall on first attempt.

 6 Now read through all your sentences and think about ways in which you could develop these using your Trigger quotes, further examples, and noting strengths and weaknesses.

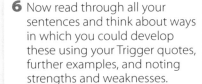 **5** Attempt to write one clear sentence to define each Trigger.

 4 When you are confident enough, order the Triggers into a list as you may do in an examination situation.

Specification Link

Religion necessary for personal growth with reference to: collective unconscious; individuation; archetypes; the God within.

AO1

What is ... Knowledge and understanding ?

This is the skill that involves *selecting* the relevant and appropriate information, *organising* it and then *presenting* it through a *personal explanation* that may involve the use of supporting *evidence* and *examples*.

Hume claimed we hide our true self behind masks. We create an image of ourselves to meet people's expectations.

❝TRIGGER QUOTES❞

The form of the world into which a person is born is already inborn in him, as a virtual image. **(C. Jung)**

Gods are personifications of unconscious contents, for they reveal themselves to us through the unconscious activity of the psyche. **(C. Jung)**

The religious images/symbols are (according to Jung) the means by which human beings discover both what they are and what they are capable of becoming. **(M. Palmer)**

Theme 2E: Carl Jung

Jung's explanation of religious belief

- ☐ Whereas Freud saw religion as something negative – a neurosis, Jung saw it as something **positive** – something necessary for **personal growth**.
- ☐ Jung agreed with Freud that we have repressed memories in our **personal unconscious**. However, Jung also thought that in addition to the personal unconscious there is the **collective unconscious**.
- ☐ The collective unconscious is **universal**, shared by the whole human race.
- ☐ It consists of **primordial images/ideas** that derive from our **ancestral past**. Therefore, these images/ideas are not from the person's own past experiences but from early human history and even **pre-human experiences**.
- ☐ They can shape our behaviour and evoke deep emotions. They are **patterns of behaviour** in our subconscious, originating from past human history and shared by all.
- ☐ The word 'archetype' means '**original pattern**'. They are part of our psyche and **unlearned**. Though they are **not images as such**, they give rise to images in the conscious mind.
- ☐ Jung saw these shared past experiences that subconsciously influence us as represented by the **symbols and myths** that can be found across all cultures.
- ☐ Often they are represented in the form of **archetypal figures** such as the wise old man or villain.
- ☐ These figures are not themselves the archetype but are the concrete images that have **crystallised** to represent the actual archetype (pattern of behaviour).
- ☐ Although they are limitless, Jung identified **four key ones**:

Archetype	What they represent
The persona	All the different social masks we wear among different groups and in different situations.
The shadow	The suppressed unconscious portion of the personality. It is often a darker side of our character that we prefer not to reveal.
The anima & the animus	Inner attitudes that take on the characteristics of the opposite sex and which are repressed as they develop a gender identity. The anima – the woman in the unconscious of every man. The animus – the man in the unconscious of every woman.
The self	The midpoint of the personality balancing the conscious and the unconscious. It represents harmony and balance.

- ☐ According to Jung, we struggle to find our **true self** because our ego gets fused to a certain person that we create to meet people's expectations. By playing with different archetypes, we find other ways of being and in order to be our true selves we must integrate these traits into our consciousness.
- ☐ **Integration** brings wholeness and balance. This process is called **individuation**.
- ☐ It is the symbols of the archetypes that help achieve this and these symbols are the images, dogmas and rites that form **religious tradition**.

- Therefore, **religion** is an important means of achieving true self.
- Individuation can be seen as a religious quest – to find the '**God within**'. God is an expression of a deep 'inner' reality or being.
- Jung was unclear as to whether or not God was an objective reality. For Jung, 'God' is an archetype in the psyche representing **wholeness**.

Supportive evidence and challenges

- Like Freud, Jung derived his theories from **personal experience** and **clinical observations**.
- Jung believed that archetypes were the means by which **dreams** could be interpreted.
- The process of realising true self was aided by religion, so religion was seen as **positive** because of the stories, symbols and archetypes it conveyed. However, it was seen as unhelpful when it focused on doctrinal correctness.
- Religion drew human beings towards **psychic wholeness** because of the stories of self-discovery and symbolic meanings it contains.
- He saw the First World War as a time when people became **disconnected** with humanity and spirituality.
- This in turn led to a **decline in religion** and the accompanying religious symbols – so removing the very things that projected the archetypes and would have contributed to the process of wholeness and balance.
- With those things absent, Jung argued that **psychoneurosis** results. There is disharmony between consciousness and unconsciousness that stops people realising their true self.
- He saw the **Asian meditation** tradition leading to enlightenment (nibbana/nirvana) similar to the idea of the Self archetype. It involved a search for the source of all existence, the psyche itself, and so was an aid to individuation.
- In contrast, Jung viewed the **Western mind** as more in search of an outer reality and so was less helpful. He felt that organised religion had caused many religious symbols to just become objects and so they had lost their meaning and power.
- **Surveys** on mental health, happiness and social benefits show a positive rating for those who are religious, supporting the claim that religion aids wholeness. Religion offers meaning to life and freedom of fear of death so is seen as a source of **comfort**.
- However, Jung's claims about archetypes and the collective unconscious cannot be demonstrated by **empirical evidence**. He relied on clinical techniques rather than a scientific methodology.
- There is no way to verify that the collective unconscious contains the archetypes. His theory is consistent with whatever images human beings construct and is therefore **unfalsifiable**.
- The fact that parallel imagery can be found across myths and religions of some cultures does not establish a **similarity of cause**. Alternative explanations could account for the similarities, e.g. as conformity to culture.
- Michael Palmer points out that Jung does not provide any **criterion** by which to distinguish one archetypal image from another.
- Neither are God-images **innate**, though Jung's theory assumes they are.
- For many religious believers, **religious experiences** are not just stemming from the mind. They have a belief in an existing external being. Jung appears agnostic about the existence of an external God.
- Jesus is seen more as an archetype than a historical person. For Jung, it is the symbol and the **psychic experience** that is important

Specification Link

Supportive evidence, including recognition of religion as a source of comfort and promotion of positive personal and social mindsets arising from religious belief. Challenges including lack of empirical evidence for Jungian concepts and reductionist views regarding religious belief arising from acceptance of Jung's ideas.

Quick Revision

Make your own table in which you describe each of the four key archetypes in your own words. This will help you with an exam question asking you to examine Jung's views.

⁶TRIGGER QUOTES⁹

The European seeks to raise himself above this world, while the Indian likes to turn back into the material depths of nature. **(C. Jung)**

... my observations ... prove only the existence of an archetypal image of the Deity which, to my mind, is the most we can assert psychologically about God. **(G. Jung)**

Jung borrowed Otto's term 'numinous' and extended its meaning ... by conferring a numinous quality upon the experience of the archetype. **(H. Ellenberger)**

A resemblance between effects does not establish a similarity in causes.

The AO2 skills of evaluation and critical analysis mean engaging with the controversies surrounding a subject. This is more than merely describing or listing the points made about a controversy. To achieve this, one weighs up strengths and weaknesses of various sides and takes a position. On the right are three controversies for each issue – you can engage in these by extending their arguments (adding examples, quotes or other details), weighing up their strengths and weaknesses, and coming to a conclusion.

⁶TRIGGER QUOTES⁹

In Jung's view religions are indispensable spiritual supports, whereas in Freud's they are illusory crutches. **(T. Szasz)**

The God-image is the expression of an underlying experience of something which I cannot attain to by intellectual means. **(C. Jung)**

[Jung was] ... seemingly indifferent to the striving for truth that lies at the heart of religious aspirations. **(E. Fromm)**

[Jung] ... rediscovered the religious and the sacred and got rid of an overwhelming rationalism. **(R. Hostie)**

Quick Revision

Often Freud is presented as negative towards religion whilst Jung is seen as positive. Make a list of (i) Freud's positive aspects of religion and (ii) Jung's negative aspects of religion.

This will help you in evaluative questions by examining the opposite views to that which are generally argued for.

Issue:

The extent to which Jung was more positive than Freud about the idea of God

Three evaluative controversies!

☐ **Controversy 1: *Don't Freud and Jung have similar views?***
They both agree that **neurosis** is the result of repression and that repressed memories are in the unconscious. Both derive their theories from personal experience and clinical observations. However, Freud saw religion as a mental illness – a neurosis that needed therapy to remove it. In contrast, Jung saw the role of religion as something very positive and necessary for **personal growth**. For Freud, **symbols** were a way people used to avoid reality, whilst Jung saw religious images as images of the deeper self and a means by which to achieve individuation.

☐ **Controversy 2: *Did Jung believe in God more than Freud?***
Many might answer this by replying 'It all depends on what you mean by God'. The traditional understanding has been to view God as an **externally existing being**, but for Jung God is more about a **deep 'inner' reality**, and for Freud, God is a creation of the human mind. Jung is more positive in that he sees God is an expression of the collective unconscious, and the **Self archetype** creates the same symbolism that has always expressed deity. A religious experience is seen as an experience with the Self. Freud sees religion as just a sexual neurosis. Jung never actually denied that God exists and some have seen individuation as having parallels with the idea of human beings having a spiritual aspect or imprint as part of their being.

☐ **Controversy 3: *Is Jung just as negative about religion as Freud?***
Jung is usually described as someone who presents a very positive view of religion. He sees God as a reality from the deepest part of the human **collective unconscious**. Indeed, he sees it as an essential activity of human beings – the means in which to integrate the unconscious and the conscious mind. However, he did view all religions to be collective **mythologies** and so many traditional religions might regard that as negative, since it could imply that they were imaginary. For instance, Jesus was seen as just a symbol for something else – an **example of an archetype**. This seems to deny Jesus as a historical person. Whereas Freud saw religions as delusionary and evil, Jung saw them merely as a tool to tap into the self.

Sp⚬tlight: **Evaluative judgements**

This section contains a special insight that you can use to form a judgement.

Is neurosis just as much an element of Jung's theory about religion as it is of Freud's? Freud certainly sees religion as a neurosis – the result of the conflict between the conscious and unconscious mind, whereby the individual represses impulses and past associations. However, Jung also recognised a relation between religion and neurosis – tension between the ego and the unconscious. But Jung, unlike Freud, saw it as something purposeful because it provides an opportunity to be conscious of who we are as opposed to who we think we are.

Issue:

To what extent are critiques of empirical approaches effective critiques of Jungian views of religion?

Spot the Triggers!
The words in blue are Triggers – key words and phrases that can help you remember knowledge and understanding in this area.

■ **Controversy 1: *What type of empirical evidence can investigate the collective unconscious?***

The term empirical evidence usually refers to **direct observation or experience** which can be assessed both in terms of quality and quantity. Jung did claim to give some evidence for the collective unconscious when he investigated the **common symbols** of myths and legends as well as identifying common ideas and ethics across numerous religions. These involve observations and analysis that are quantitative and qualitative. However, the collective unconscious raises the problem that it is private to the observer since it involves **inner psychological states**. Although there is observation, it is **subjective** and cannot be verified. One question that then arises is – 'to what extent does that matter?'

■ **Controversy 2: *What is meant by 'real'?***

Empirical evidence and scientific methodology are required to examine what is real (reality). In this sense, reality is something **objective and not private**. However, Jung was interested in investigating the subjective experience. He was concerned about whether the subjective experience was a **genuine experience**. It was not about a reality separate from the subject but about the state of mind that was actually being **experienced by the subject**. It is this experience that although real, is not necessarily 'real' in the empirical understanding of what reality consists of.

■ **Controversy 3: *Should Jung's views be dismissed?***

This will depend on whether you think the evidence is **persuasive**. Those who regard the empirical approach as the only type of evidence that can be accepted, although they may accept evidence for **common symbols**, the claim that these arise from a collective unconscious and archetypes will be, by necessity, considered **invalid**. Others may be persuaded by the extent to which Jung's **theory works**. For instance, psychotherapy practices achieve positive results and the Myers-Briggs Type Indicator, developed from Jung's theories, has become a popular psychometric instrument. However, there are other fields in psychology, such as cognitive and behavioural therapies, that are also successful yet are not based on Jung's understanding of the human psyche.

Jung's approach is often said to be unscientific in the methods he used to develop his theories.

TRIGGER QUOTES

[Psychic 'facts' are] useful in the context of discovery, but not in the context of justification.   **(M. Mattoon)**

A subjective feeling of the truth of an idea is no support for its being accepted as a hypothesis.   **(K. Popper)**

Although I have often been called a philosopher, I am an empiricist and adhere as such to the phenomenological standpoint.   **(C. Jung)**

Sp⬤tlight: **Evaluative judgements**

This section contains a special insight that you can use to form a judgement.

Is our sense that there is an 'objective reality' a delusion? Empirical evidence is derived from our senses but philosophy has challenged the reliability of our senses. It is often said that we could all be a brain in a vat, wired so we are deluded into thinking we are living a particular life. We could also doubt our reasoning abilities. How would we weigh up Jung's view of religion in light of these insights?

AO1 Trigger revision activity

A

ZIP

Jung's explanation of religious belief

personal unconscious	collective unconscious	wholeness	primordial images/ideas
not images as such	God within	religion	religious tradition
ancestral past	symbols and myths	true self	
positive, pre-human experiences	universal	crystallised	integration
four key ones	original pattern	patterns of behaviour	unlearned

1 Fix the zip file! There are three Triggers missing from this zip file – find them and add them in.

➡

2 There's another problem: the Triggers are out of order! Put them in the same order as they appear in the AO1 section above.

➡

3 Practise 'downloading' your zip file of Triggers from memory. See how many you can recall on first attempt.

⬇

6 Now read through your definitions and think about ways in which you could develop these using your Trigger quotes.

⬅

5 Attempt to write one clear sentence to define each Trigger.

⬅

4 When you are confident enough, order the Triggers into a list as you may do in an examination situation.

B

ZIP

Supportive evidence and challenges

1 There are no Triggers in this zip file! Find and add in the relevant Triggers.

➡

2 Now put the Triggers in the same order as they appear in the AO1 section above.

➡

3 Practise 'downloading' your zip file of Triggers from memory. See how many you can recall on first attempt.

⬇

6 Now read through your definitions and think about ways in which you could develop these using your Trigger quotes.

⬅

5 Attempt to write one clear sentence to define each Trigger.

⬅

4 When you are confident enough, order the Triggers into a list as you may do in an examination situation.

AO2 Trigger revision activity

Is Jung more positive than Freud about the idea of God?

| Similar views, symbols, personal growth, neurosis | Negative, example of archetype collective unconscious, mythologies | Believe in God, Self archetype |

1 Fix the zip file! There are two Triggers missing from this zip file – find them and add them in.

2 There's another problem: the Triggers are out of order! Put them in the same order as they appear in the AO2 section above.

3 Practise 'downloading' your zip file of Triggers from memory. See how many you can recall on first attempt.

4 When you are confident enough, order the Triggers into a list as you may do in an examination situation.

5 Attempt to write one clear sentence to define each Trigger.

6 Now read through all your sentences and think about ways in which you could develop these using your Trigger quotes, further examples, and noting strengths and weaknesses.

Should Jung's views be dismissed?

1 There are no Triggers in this zip file! Find and add in the relevant Triggers.

2 Now put the Triggers in the same order as they appear in the AO2 section above.

3 Practise 'downloading' your zip file of Triggers from memory. See how many you can recall on first attempt.

4 When you are confident enough, order the Triggers into a list as you may do in an examination situation.

5 Attempt to write one clear sentence to define each Trigger.

6 Now read through all your sentences and think about ways in which you could develop these using your Trigger quotes, further examples, and noting strengths and weaknesses.

AO1

What is ... Knowledge and understanding ?

This is the skill that involves *selecting* the relevant and appropriate information, *organising* it and then *presenting* it through a *personal explanation* that may involve the use of supporting *evidence* and *examples*.

An agnostic suspends the decision to accept or reject belief in God because metaphysics is considered to be an unknowable area.

❛TRIGGER QUOTES❜

I have never been an atheist in the sense of denying the existence of God. I think generally ... an agnostic would be the most correct description of my mind. **(C. Darwin)**

It is a short step from the thought that the different religions cannot all be true, although they all claim to be, to the thought that in all probability none of them is true. **(J. Hick)**

Theme 2F: **Atheism**

Atheism and agnosticism

- ▫ The lack of a deity in the **Asian religions** of Jainism, Buddhism and Taoism has led some to regard these as the earliest examples of atheism, dating from the sixth century BCE.
- ▫ However, this may be a **misunderstanding** of these religions and stem from their rejection of the idea of a creator god.
- ▫ The word 'atheistic' in ancient Greek meant '**disrespecting the local gods**' so did not deny belief in other gods.
- ▫ Traditionally, the first atheist is usually identified as the Greek poet **Diagoras of Melos** who lived in the fifth century BCE, but it is not clear whether he was an atheist in the Ancient Greek sense or whether he thought there were no gods at all.
- ▫ The 18th century saw **two movements** that challenged belief in God; the Age of Enlightenment and the French Revolution.
- ▫ In the 20th century **whole states** emerged as atheistic such as the Soviet Union and China. A feature of the 21st century is a more **militant** form of atheism – 'New Atheism' or 'Antitheism'.
- ▫ The **differences** between agnosticism and atheism:

Weak atheism	Does not believe in God but equally does not assert that no God exists	'I don't believe that God exists but tell me why you do believe in God?'
Strong atheism	Asserts that God does not exist	'God does not exist, and here are my reasons. So why do you believe in God?'
Weak agnosticism	God may or may not exist but judgement has to be withheld until evidence becomes available	'I don't know whether God exists or not, but maybe you do.'
Strong agnosticism	It is impossible to know whether or not God exists	'I don't know whether God exists or not, and neither do you.'

- ▫ Modern usage of the term 'agnostic' is applied to people who think that God's existence and his non-existence are equally probable. This usage reflects the **postmodern** idea of rejecting absolute certainties about knowledge.

Criticisms of religion by New Atheism

- ▫ The attack on the **Twin Towers** was one of the triggers for New Atheism, a movement that saw not just religious extremists but religion in general as dangerous and deluded.
- ▫ Four people (**the Four Horsemen**) have been the key voices of New Atheism – Sam Harris, Richard Dawkins, Daniel Dennett and Christopher Hitchens.
- ▫ New Atheism claims that faith and religion are irrational. Religious people are seen as **non-thinking** and infantile.

- They accuse adults of **forcing belief** in God upon children to be brought up to believe unquestioningly. Such non-thinking leads to **fanaticism**. Atheists have done evil things but not because of atheism but for other reasons.
- New Atheism focuses on natural selection to explain design, and views religionists as believing in the '**God of the gaps**'. It claims that the religious view of reality is deficient and impoverished. It is not a choice between **God or chaos**.
- Religion impedes scientific progress since blind faith and religious fundamentalism **subvert science** by running away from evidence.
- It teaches people not to change their mind and so **saps intellect**.
- Dawkins views the 'infection' of religion as the misfiring of **two survival mechanisms**: the tendency to obey elders and the tendency to assign meaning and purpose to animals and objects.
- New Atheism rejects the idea of the **supernatural** and indeed any beliefs that are held without evidence. Therefore, they are not just a-theists but also a-toothfairyists, etc.
- It **depicts God** as a misogynist, homophobic, racist, megalomaniac, sadomasochist and a capricious malevolent bully.

Religious responses to New Atheism

- New Atheism is accused of attacking lazy **caricatures** or degenerate forms of religion and ignores the mainstream reality.
- It depicts science and religion as offering competing explanations and that only scientific explanations are valid. However, **John Polkinghorne** sees no competition or conflict and argues that there are **different levels of explanation** that need weaving together to provide a comprehensive whole.
- For instance, a scientific description of the world may involve the Big Bang and evolution. **Religious descriptions** may refer to a process involving direct action or God creating and working through natural forces.
- The notions of **value and meaning** lie beyond the scope of natural sciences since they are non-empirical.
- **Alister McGrath** points out that both science and religion involve showing that there are good reasons for thinking something is right, without having total confirmation. There is a difference between 'a total absence of supporting evidence' and 'an absence of totally supporting evidence'.
- This has led to some religious groups becoming more unwavering to their set of beliefs and more vociferous in their **opposition** to atheistic trends in society. They try to **motivate the electorate** on particular social issues, e.g. abortion.
- New Atheism has also given a public platform for discussion about Christianity. The Church has been prompted to recover an **apologetic tradition**.
- TV and **social media** have opened the debate to a wider audience, as, for example, the 'Atheist Bus' campaign which was copied in other countries beyond the UK.

TRIGGER QUOTES

When a man is freed of religion he has a better chance to live a normal and wholesome life. **(S. Freud)**

We are all atheists about most of the gods that humanity has ever believed in. Some of us just go one god further **(R. Dawkins)**

Quick Revision

In your own words, give reasons why an agnostic (i) could and (ii) could never become an atheist. In your answer make sure you take into account (i) the different understandings of the word 'atheist' and (ii) the different understandings of the word 'agnostic'. This will help you answer exam questions on this area.

Specification Link

Religious responses to the challenge of New Atheism: rejection by religious groups of New Atheist claims regarding incompatibility of science and religion; increase in fundamental religious activity relating to morality and community; increase in religious apologists in media.

TRIGGER QUOTES

Those who believe absurdities will commit atrocities. **(Voltaire)**

Faith is the great cop-out, the great excuse to evade the need to think and evaluate evidence ... Faith is not allowed to justify itself by argument. **(R. Dawkins)**

By all means let's be open-minded, but not so open-minded that our brains drop out. **(R. Dawkins)**

As it happens, no atheist should call himself or herself one. The term already sells a pass to theists, because it invites debate on their ground. A more appropriate term is 'naturalist'. **(A. C. Grayling)**

New Atheism says that religion is both deluded and dangerous. It is seen as a threat to society.

❝TRIGGER QUOTES❞

The very existence of the capacity for rational thought is surely a pointer: not downwards to chance and necessity, but upwards to an intelligent source of that capacity. **(J. Lennox)**

The scientific explanation neither conflicts nor competes with the agent explanation. **(J. Lennox)**

The most incomprehensible thing about the universe is that it is comprehensible. **(A. Einstein)**

AO2

What is ... Evaluation and critical analysis ❓■

The AO2 skills of evaluation and critical analysis mean engaging with the controversies surrounding a subject. This is more than merely describing or listing the points made about a controversy. To achieve this, one weighs up strengths and weaknesses of various sides and takes a position. On the right are three controversies for each issue – you can engage in these by extending their arguments (adding examples, quotes or other details), weighing up their strengths and weaknesses, and coming to a conclusion.

❝TRIGGER QUOTES❞

Only religious faith is a strong enough force to motivate such utter madness in otherwise sane and decent people. **(R. Dawkins)**

For God so loved the world, that he gave his only begotten Son, that whosoever believeth in him will believeth in anything. Hitchens 3:16 **(C. Hitchens)**

You are right in speaking of the moral foundations of science, but you cannot turn around and speak of the scientific foundations of morality. **(A. Einstein)**

Issue:
The success of atheistic arguments against religious belief

Three evaluative controversies!

☐ **Controversy 1:** *Is New Atheism accurate about religion and religious teaching being the cause of much violence?*
It is true that the terrorist attack on the Twin Towers was perpetrated by **religious extremists**. It was this event that galvanised the New Atheist movement. Dawkins also points to the **Crusades**, the Inquisition, suicide bombings and various religious wars as evidence of the mayhem that religion has caused. However, most religious believers would claim that such actions are of people who **live inconsistently** with the religious teachings about non-violence, love and forgiveness. New Atheists also ignore violence from atheists such as **Lenin** who tried to eradicate religious belief.

☐ **Controversy 2:** *Should New Atheism be more critical of science?*
New Atheism maintains that science has the potential to explain everything and that only scientific explanations are valid. Such a view is called **scientism**. Indeed, Dawkins argues that science has disproved God, and the need for religious explanations has become redundant. But surely science does have **limitations**. It cannot pronounce on non-empirical notions such as value and meaning. New Atheists claim that science can tell us what is morally right on the grounds that **moral values** are about promoting human well-being. But is that what morality is about? The scientific method draws upon reasonable **probabilities** rather than certainties, yet New Atheists seem to deny any other possibility can occur.

☐ **Controversy 3:** *Has New Atheism done more to promote religion than destroy it?*
New Atheism has certainly led to much **public discussion** and debate, including via TV and social media. Religious beliefs have been challenged and as a result have led to a **response** by the religious faiths. The challenges have been focused and led to **clarity of areas** of disagreement. McGrath commented that we quickly abandon what no one shows the ability to defend. Religion continues to **wane and grow** in different parts of the world, but New Atheism has allowed for a more authentic public discussion and has itself come under attack from other atheists.

Sp●tlight: **Evaluative judgements**
This section contains a special insight that you can use to form a judgement.

Is atheism the only challenge to belief in God? New Atheism has had a high profile and resulted in much discussion about belief in God. Indeed, there are a variety of different types of atheism. For instance, Protest atheism sees God as morally corrupt because of the amount of senseless suffering that is in the world. Challenges to traditional belief have found voice from amongst the Church itself. For instance, an Anglican priest, Don Cupitt, presented a TV series that gave rise to the 'Sea of Faith' movement which seeks to 'explore and promote religious faith as a human creation'.

Issue:

The extent to which religious responses to New Atheism have been successful

◻ **Controversy 1:** *Is faith nothing but blind belief?*

New Atheism depicts a religious believer as someone who is **irrational** and has been brought up to believe unquestioningly. It is something that adults have forced on them as children and it is this **non-thinking** that leads to dangerous fanaticism. However, this denies the historical **evidence** for a faith. For example, in Christianity there is a case to be answered regards the resurrection of Jesus, and Muhammad receiving the Qu'ran. There is rational debate about the evidence even though both sides may disagree. It is claimed that faith is not blind but is more about acting on what you have **good reason** to believe is true.

◻ **Controversy 2:** *Does science reach agreed conclusions?*

New Atheism portrays science as the **ultimate source** of explaining everything – the definitive answer to all questions. Religions are seen as promoting ignorance and **running away** from evidence. In contrast, science gives clear answers from evidence that automatically leads to only one conclusion. It is true that there are a variety of different religious beliefs but there are also a variety of **different conclusions** based on scientific evidence. For instance, such areas as the origin of life, consciousness and multi-universes are far from agreed by the scientific fraternity. Indeed, science never gives certainties only **probabilities**, since the scientific method rests on falsification rather than verification

◻ **Controversy 3:** *Is the conflict between science and religion that New Atheism presents valid?*

Religion is seen by New Atheists as something that goes against all scientific principles. Yet it cannot be denied that there are eminent **scientists** who also hold a religious belief and see no conflict between the two. Stephen Gould views science and religion as **mutually exclusive**, the former dealing with the natural world and the latter with questions of a spiritual nature. Others, like John Polkinghorne, view science and religion as offering **different levels of explanation** that need weaving together. Ian Barbour favours **integration** arguing that natural theology uses the results of the natural sciences as premises in its arguments (e.g. the cosmological argument).

Is faith blind belief in the face of evidence or acting on what you have good reason to believe is true?

❝ TRIGGER QUOTES ❞

Faith, being belief that isn't based on evidence, is the principal vice of any religion. **(R. Dawkins)**

Religion is a culture of faith; science is a culture of doubt. **(R. Feynman)**

One of the bad effects of religion is that it teaches us that it is a virtue to be satisfied with not understanding. **(R. Dawkins)**

Spotlight: Evaluative judgements

This section contains a special insight that you can use to form a judgement.

Can God be proved? Many from the Abrahamic faiths would argue that God is not a physical object so is not open to investigation by means of the senses. But even our senses are unreliable so can anything be proved? The arguments for God's existence were never claimed to be proofs but were to demonstrate the coherence of faith. Recent defences of the traditional arguments attempt to show them as justifiable rather than proven. However, Dawkins comments that there is 'certainly no reason to suppose that, just because God can be neither proved nor disproved, his probability of existence is 50 per cent'.

SCIENCE RELIGION

The signpost points science and religion as going in different directions. But are they incompatible? Is a scientific explanation the only valid explanation?

AO1 Trigger revision activity

A
ZIP

Atheism and agnosticism

1 There are no Triggers in this zip file! Find and add in the relevant Triggers.

→

2 Now put the Triggers in the same order as they appear in the AO1 section above.

→

3 Practise 'downloading' your zip file of Triggers from memory. See how many you can recall on first attempt.

6 Now read through your definitions and think about ways in which you could develop these using your Trigger quotes.

←

5 Attempt to write one clear sentence to define each Trigger.

←

4 When you are confident enough, order the Triggers into a list as you may do in an examination situation.

B
ZIP

Religious responses to New Atheism

depicts God	nepotism	saps intellect
Aquinas	God or chaos	Twin Towers
subvert science	non-thinking	two survival mechanisms
forcing belief	extra-terrestrial	

1 Find the unhelpful Triggers! **This zip file contains several inappropriate or irrelevant Triggers**. Find these and replace them with the real Triggers from the AO1 section.

→

2 There's another problem: the Triggers are out of order! Put them in the same order as they appear in the AO1 section above.

→

3 Practise 'downloading' your zip file of Triggers from memory. See how many you can recall on first attempt.

6 Now read through your definitions and think about ways in which you could develop these using your Trigger quotes.

←

5 Attempt to write one clear sentence to define each Trigger.

←

4 When you are confident enough, order the Triggers into a list as you may do in an examination situation.

AO2 Trigger revision activity

A
ZIP

Is New Atheism convincing?

1 There are no Triggers in this zip file! Find and add in the relevant Triggers.

2 Now put the Triggers in the same order as they appear in the AO2 section above.

3 Practise 'downloading' your zip file of Triggers from memory. See how many you can recall on first attempt.

6 Now read through all your sentences and think about ways in which you could develop these using your Trigger quotes, further examples, and noting strengths and weaknesses.

5 Attempt to write one clear sentence to define each Trigger.

4 When you are confident enough, order the Triggers into a list as you may do in an examination situation.

B
ZIP

Does science oppose religion?

erratic, good reason, blind belief, evidence, non-thinking

scientists, conflict, mutually exclusive, segregation, different levels of explanation

probabilities, running away, different conclusions, original source

1 Find the unhelpful Triggers! **This zip file contains several inappropriate or irrelevant Triggers**. Find these and replace them with the real Triggers from the AO2 section.

2 There's another problem: the Triggers are out of order! Put them in the same order as they appear in the AO2 section above.

3 Practise 'downloading' your zip file of Triggers from memory. See how many you can recall on first attempt.

6 Now read through all your sentences and think about ways in which you could develop these using your Trigger quotes, further examples, and noting strengths and weaknesses.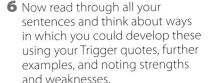

5 Attempt to write one clear sentence to define each Trigger.

4 When you are confident enough, order the Triggers into a list as you may do in an examination situation.

Theme 3D: Religious practice and faith

Value for religious community

Specification Link

Value for religious community including: affirmation of belief system; promotion of faith value system; strengthening cohesion of religious community.

AO1

What is ... Knowledge and understanding?

This is the skill that involves *selecting* the relevant and appropriate information, *organising* it and then *presenting* it through a *personal explanation* that may involve the use of supporting *evidence* and *examples*.

Is worship a religious experience?

TRIGGER QUOTES

But for many people at many times the 'fair beauty of the Lord' is revealed chiefly or only while they worship Him together.
(C. S. Lewis)

Ritual is probably the most common source of religious experience for the majority of people. **(M. Momen)**

- ☐ **Religious practice** such as ritual, religious ceremonies and festivals, and religious duties of daily life, can be influenced by religious experiences or even trigger them.
- ☐ The move from a belief-that to a **belief-in** is often brought about by a personal religious experience.
- ☐ The religious experiences of **others** can also be a source of one's own faith.
- ☐ Many founders of religious traditions claim to have had a **revelation** through religious experience.
- ☐ Religious experiences are seen as confirmation and affirmation of the **authority** of a key figure in a religion. Think of a key religious figure in the religion you are studying and how their religious experience gained them authority amongst their followers.
- ☐ When a religious community comes together for **collective worship** then these occasions can strengthen the community spiritually and provide opportunity for further religious experiences.
- ☐ In Christian **charismatic worship** there is the expectation that the Holy Spirit will be present amongst the worshippers.
- ☐ Reading and preaching of the **sacred text** can lead to a special kind of communal experience since many religious traditions consider their scriptures as the revealed word of God.
- ☐ In Christianity the **Eucharist** ritual is a time when the mystery of another dimension to life can be experienced.
- ☐ The celebration of a past religious experience through **festivals or pilgrimage** creates a greater sense of **unity** and establishes a common identity and purpose.

Religion	Festival	Event it celebrates
Buddhism	Wesak	The birth, enlightenment and death of Gautama Buddha
Christianity	Easter	The resurrection of Jesus
Hinduism	Kumbh Mela	Dhanvantari dropping the pot of nectar to earth at four places
Islam	Ramadan	The Qur'an first revealed to Muhammad
Judaism	Pesach	The events of Passover
Sikhism	Valsakhi	The formation of the Khalsa

- ☐ **Initiation** into a faith usually takes place publicly and involves some statement of commitment.
- ☐ Opportunities to renew **commitment** to the faith and ideals often take place publicly, confirming their faith in front of other believers.

Religion	Commitment/rites of passage	Objects or actions
Buddhism	Monastic opportunities	Short-term monastic vows for youth – Theravada countries
Christianity	Infant baptism and confirmation or adult baptism	Sprinkling and anointing with oil or total immersion in water
Hinduism	Sacred thread	Head shaved, new clothes put on after bathing, giving of sacred thread, vows made, sometimes a second name is given
Islam	Aqeeqah	Sacrifice of an animal, reciting the adhan, shaving the baby's head
Judaism	Bar or Bat Mitzvah	Sabbath nearest 13th birthday, reading aloud of part of Torah, wearing of tefillin for first time
Sikhism	The Sikh Amrit ceremony	Double edged sword, nectar, water, reciting of five sacred texts, drinking of the water and nectar

Value for individual

- Alister Hardy set up the Religious Experience Research Unit in Oxford to compile a database of religious experiences which revealed a huge **breadth and variety** of experiences.
- When Hardy asked a question about RE to **individuals** he received many reports of religious experiences.
- His **question** was *'Have you ever been aware of or influenced by a presence or power, whether you call it God or not, which is different from your everyday self?'*
- Hardy discovered that many not involved in religious communities spoke of experiences that could be called '**religious**'.
- Hardy saw that common features of a religious experience included an awareness of **another dimension of life** which alters behaviour and changes attitudes.
- A person's own religious experiences, when God meets with that person, can be a time when doubts are removed and **faith restored**.
- The source of this experience could be **triggered** by such religious activities as prayer, meditation, the reading of sacred text, ritual or pilgrimage.
- It can also come from the **testimony** of others and their religious experience as they recount how God influenced their life.
- **Opposition** can be the cause of loss of faith; religious experience recounting how God rescued a person from a situation or gave strength to face and overcome the opposition, can restore and renew faith. Accounts of **martyrs** can inspire faith in the face of opposition.
- A religious experience can give a sense of **Divine presence**, which can enable the person to stand firm and continue despite threats of persecution.
- Individuals participating in **festivals** in their religion have opportunity for reflection in order to develop a closer relationship with their religion.
- Individuals who **fast** offer another occasion to turn away from this world and instead focus on God.
- **Holy places** offer a place where there is a sacred meeting between the spiritual and the physical, and can trigger religious experiences.
- Religious experiences are seen by many people to help to overcome stress and **anxiety**.
- It reminds them of a greater meaning and **purpose to life** – something that religious rituals may not do for them.

TIP

Spot the Triggers!
The words in blue are Triggers – key words and phrases that can help you remember knowledge and understanding in this area.

Specification Link

Value for individual including faith restoring; strengthening faith in face of opposition; renewal of commitment to religious ideals and doctrines.

Quick Revision

Selecting examples of religious experience that are related to the world religion that you have been studying, explain how each of the values for religious community and for individuals listed in the specification can be illustrated from that religion. This will help you answer questions about the value of religious experiences for the religious community and for the individual.

The façade of Westminster Abbey showing 20th-century martyrs.

❝TRIGGER QUOTES❞

We must judge the tree by its fruit. The best fruits of the religious experience are the best things history has to offer ... flights of charity, devotion, trust, patience, and bravery ... **(W. James)**

The results of religious experiences are the only reliable basis for judging whether it is a genuine experience of the divine.

(W. James)

AO2

What is ...
Evaluation and critical analysis ?

The AO2 skills of evaluation and critical analysis mean engaging with the controversies surrounding a subject. This is more than merely describing or listing the points made about a controversy. To achieve this, one weighs up strengths and weaknesses of various sides and takes a position. On the right are three controversies for each issue – you can engage in these by extending their arguments (adding examples, quotes or other details), weighing up their strengths and weaknesses, and coming to a conclusion.

To what extent is the Eucharist service a religious experience?

⟨ TRIGGER QUOTES ⟩

Issue:

The impact of religious experiences upon religious belief and practice

Three evaluative controversies!

- **Controversy 1: *Are** prayer/meditation/mantras **both a religious practice and a religious experience?***
  These would seem a clear example of a religious practice that can be a religious experience. **Communication** with a transcendent realm is said to take place – both speaking to the divine and listening to the 'voice' of the divine. William James described prayer as 'the very soul and essence of religion'. However, the **repetition** of prayers can be rote and **mechanical**. Can repeating the Mool Mantra or the Lord's Prayer really lead to, or be a religious experience? If they are not, then what has to be the nature of prayer for it to be such or does it more **depend on God** and not us?

- **Controversy 2: *Do religious experiences cast doubt rather than affirm religious belief?***
  Often key religious figures have a religious experience at the start of their ministry that challenged rather than affirmed their beliefs. It is this religious experience that is seen as **confirming and affirming** their message. St Paul and his conversion experience on the **Damascus Road** is an example. But what about when people have revelations that seem to **counter** other revelations that people have had? (E.g. The Qur'an revealed to Muhammad.) How is it possible to decide which if any is the **correct revelation**?

- **Controversy 3: *Does religious experience always lead to strengthening cohesion of a religious community?***
  Religious communities **recall past events**, often of religious experiences of founders, through festival and ritual. This undoubtedly gives followers a common **identity and purpose**. In the same way, collective worship can be a religious experience that strengthens the community spiritually. However, religious experiences can also be the cause of division. There can develop **spiritual superiority** with those who have certain religious experiences. For instance, in the Christian tradition some traditions regard an experience of the **Holy Spirit** (filled with the Holy Spirit) as a necessary religious experience to be a Christian.

Spotlight: Evaluative judgements

This section contains a special insight that you can use to form a judgement.

If religious experiences strengthen faith for individuals and communities, why do so many report not having them? Does this mean that they are not committed enough? Or that they are mistaken in the power behind their religion? If a person has a religious experience and if there is a God, then it seems reasonable to believe that God could affirm the experience with such certainty that there could be no doubt. What of experiences that seemed contrary to the faith? Would that mean a change of faith?

Issue:

Whether religious communities are entirely dependent on religious experiences

- **Controversy 1: *Are there *dangers* of a religion that depends entirely on religious experiences?***

  If religion is concerned with belief and worship of God or gods then it would seem necessary that there be some **communication** between the believer and the God or gods. This, by nature, would be a form of religious experience. If the worship is not of a personal being such as in some forms of Buddhism, then through meditation there is still a religious experience. However, modern views about religious language, literary sources and psychology have raised doubts about the **interpretations** of those past and present religious experiences. And if our own religious experiences can be explained by **psychology**, then are they too not valid? In such cases what would remain of the religion?

- **Controversy 2: *Are religious experiences the most important aspect of being religious?***

  A lack of religious experience would suggest that God/the divine is just **God of the past** and not of all times and places. Surely religious experiences should be the vital aspect of the experience of religious communities. However, there may be debate as to whether all forms of religious experience are **equally important** or whether it is just particular ones: for example, those experienced by the founders of the religion, or perhaps those experienced by present followers of the religion. Others may see the practices and ritual of the religion the most important aspect. This may include certain **rules** of behaviour and conduct. In such cases, it is the living out the faith in a **practical way** that is the most important aspect.

- **Controversy 3: *Are religious experiences the only way that a religious belief can be confirmed?***

  Certainly, religious experiences both of the past, including **the founders**, and those of **present-day** followers are ways that confirm a religious belief. However, the more mundane matters of religion, such as **buildings**, rituals and set prayers are actually what keep religions **alive** and passed on to the next generation – not dynamic experiences. However, it could be argued that all of these **mundane practices** ARE religious experiences!

Sp●tlight: **Evaluative judgements**

This section contains a special insight that you can use to form a judgement.

Doesn't a religious experience have to be first hand not second hand? Indeed, some religious traditions really focus on religious experiences whilst for others they are seen more as a side-show. To what extent is someone else's religious experience valid for you? Religious experiences are personal, private and subjective. You cannot experience what they experience. Indeed, can you even understand it since it involves the 'wholly other'? Does this not suggest that only your own religious experiences can be of value?

‹TRIGGER QUOTES ›

... that Jesus actually walked out of the grave with the same body that went into it, leaving an empty tomb to astonish all, was probably a legend that developed over the course of the first century ... **(R. Carrier)**

[for Teresa] the mysticism is demystified, and mystical experience as such is accorded no particular authority. Its authority . . . has to be displayed in the shape of the vocation of which it is part. **(R. Williams)**

AO1 Trigger revision activity

A

ZIP

Value for religious community

Initiation	unit	revolution	collection
charismatic worship	sacred text	belief-in	others
Eucharist	religious practice	festivals or	
confinement	authority	pilgrimage	

1 Find the unhelpful Triggers! **This zip file contains several inappropriate or irrelevant Triggers**. Find these and replace them with the real Triggers from the AO1 section.

2 There's another problem: the Triggers are out of order! Put them in the same order as they appear in the AO1 section above.

3 Practise 'downloading' your zip file of Triggers from memory. See how many you can recall on first attempt.

6 Now read through your definitions and think about ways in which you could develop these using your Trigger quotes.

5 Attempt to write one clear sentence to define each Trigger.

4 When you are confident enough, order the Triggers into a list as you may do in an examination situation.

B

ZIP

Value for individual

Breadth and variety	another dimension of life	opposition	fast
individuals	faith restored	martyrs	Holy places
question	triggered	Divine presence	anxiety
religious	testimony	festivals	purpose to life

1 Here is your zip file of portable Triggers.

2 Practise 'downloading' your zip file of Triggers from memory. See how many you can recall on first attempt.

3 When you are confident enough, order the Triggers into a list as you may do in an examination situation.

5 Now read through your descriptions and think about ways in which you could develop these using your Trigger quotes.

4 Attempt to write one clear sentence to define each Trigger.

Why Trigger?
Remember, your Triggers are to help you transfer your knowledge and understanding in a manageable, efficient and portable manner.

TIP

AO2 Trigger revision activity

 A ZIP

Strengthening cohesion of a religious community?

depend on God, communication, manual, superstition, prayer/meditation/mantras

confirming and affirming, Jerusalem Road, counter, correct revelation

Holy Spirit, recall past sins, spiritual superiority, strengthening cohesion, identity and purpose

1 Find the unhelpful Triggers! **This zip file contains several inappropriate or irrelevant Triggers**. Find these and replace them with the real Triggers from the AO2 section.

2 There's another problem: the Triggers are out of order! Put them in the same order as they appear in the AO2 section above.

3 Practise 'downloading' your zip file of Triggers from memory. See how many you can recall on first attempt.

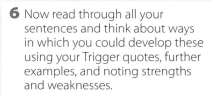

6 Now read through all your sentences and think about ways in which you could develop these using your Trigger quotes, further examples, and noting strengths and weaknesses.

5 Attempt to write one clear sentence to define each Trigger.

4 When you are confident enough, order the Triggers into a list as you may do in an examination situation.

B ZIP

Are religious communities dependent on religious experiences?

dangers, communications, interpretations, psychology

God of the past, equally important, rules, practical way

the founders, present day, buildings, alive, mundane practices

1 Here is your zip file of portable Triggers.

2 Practise 'downloading' your zip file of Triggers from memory. See how many you can recall on first attempt.

3 When you are confident enough, order the Triggers into a list as you may do in an examination situation.

5 Now read through all your sentences and think about ways in which you could develop these using your Trigger quotes, further examples, and noting strengths and weaknesses.

4 'Double-click' each Trigger in your memory – what can you say about an evaluative point of view in a clear sentence? Write this down. Do this for each Trigger in turn.

REVISION TIP

Using Trigger quotes
When you choose the Trigger quotes that you wish to use make sure that you explain how they are relevant.

Religious experience

AO1

What is ...
Knowledge and
understanding **?**

This is the skill that involves *selecting* the relevant and appropriate information, *organising* it and then *presenting* it through a *personal explanation* that may involve the use of supporting *evidence* and *examples*.

The train has stopped for reasons other than the boy on the track. Is this just a beneficial coincidence or is God involved?

Spot the Triggers!
The words in blue are Triggers – key words and phrases that can help you remember knowledge and understanding in this area.

TIP

Theme 3E: **Miracles**

Definitions of 'miracle'

- The word 'miracle is derived from the Latin word for '**wonder**' and its main characteristic is that it should provoke wonder, usually because it is unusual or extraordinary.
- **St Aquinas** believed that everything that existed had a nature (i.e. the things that it is able to do). A miracle is when something takes place that is not the normal part of **the nature of things**.
- He distinguished between **three kinds of miracles**:

The event described	An example
God does something which nature could never do	The sun going back on its course across the sky
God does something which nature can do but not in the usual order	Someone living after death
God does something that nature does but without the operation of the principles of nature	Someone instantly cured of an illness that would naturally take much longer to cure

- By the 17th century, and the time of **David Hume**, the behaviour of things became expressed in terms of the **laws of nature** or natural laws, rather than in terms of their nature and the powers they had to act.
- Hume defined a miracle as 'a **transgression of a law of nature** by a particular volition of the Deity, or by the interposition of some invisible agent' – for example, the raising of a person from the dead.
- For Hume, miracles had to break the laws of nature and have a **divine cause**.
- Some interpret Hume's definition in a **'hard' sense** in that miracles are seen as impossible since the laws of nature are regarded as unalterably uniform and cannot be broken.
- Others interpret in a **'soft' sense** where laws of nature can have exceptions. Belief in miracles in such a view will then be dependent on the credibility of the evidence.
- **Richard Swinburne** endorses Hume's view making **two additions**: (i) he replaces 'violation of a law of nature' with 'an occurrence of a non-repeatable counter-instance to a law of nature' (ii) he sees miracles as signs that contribute to a Divine purpose.
- The first addition means that the modified law is **temporary** for that one event only and the regular law of nature applies in all other circumstances.
- The second addition highlights the idea that miracles occur for a purpose and **point** to something beyond the actual event.
- In contrast to Aquinas, Hume and Swinburne, **Ray Holland** advocated the idea of **contingency miracles**.
- He defined a miracle as 'a remarkable and **beneficial coincidence** that is interpreted in a religious way'.

- In his illustration of the boy in a **toy car** trapped on the railway lines, there is a **natural explanation** for why the train driver stopped the train even though he couldn't see the boy trapped on the line. The watching mother nevertheless thanked God.
- Holland implies that only if the **person interprets** the event as a miracle can the event be called a miracle.

Why religious believers accept that miracles occur

- God's intervention in the form of a miracle is seen by some as consistent with a God who loves and is compassionate. It would be expected that God would intervene through miracles on occasions to demonstrate that **love**.
- It is probable that God would produce a revelation that could be confirmed as **authentic**. Swinburne argues that a miracle would meet this requirement.
- Miracles function as a **divine signature** for believers, confirming the authority and truth claims of a particular faith tradition.
- God answering **prayers** is another reason to believe that God would perform miracles.
- Many religions in their sacred texts record supernatural events which are seen to **vindicate** the claims of those who are accepted as God's messengers.
- In **Christianity** there are accounts in which Jesus is said to have been resurrected from the dead, which is seen by believers as confirmation that Jesus is the Son of God.
- There are examples in early **Buddhist texts** of people who claimed to have developed supernatural powers from mystical practices; later tantric practices within Buddhism are associated with experiences of the miraculous.
- Miracles play an important role in the **veneration** of Buddhist relics in Southern Asia. For example, the Somawathie Stupa in Sri Lanka.
- The fact that miracles are claimed to have occurred in different religions brings different responses from religious believers. Many claim that the only 'true' religion has 'true' miracles whilst other religions have either no miracles or '**demonic magic**' or sorcery.
- Other religious believers accept that such **diversity of miracles** supports the claim that those religions also make valid or true claims. They argue that each religion contains a valid response to **the reality of God**.
- A **personal experience** of a claimed miracle can clearly be a decisive proof to that individual that miracles happen.
- Hearing **testimonies** of others who claim to have experienced miracles can generate faith in individuals. The Roman Catholic Shrine at Lourdes attracts religious believers who believe in a God who answers prayer for healing in a miraculous way. Since 1858 it is claimed there have been 69 verified healings or cures at **Lourdes**.
- If miracles are understood in the sense of **contingency miracles** then it may not be about an action undertaken by a supernatural agent.

⟨TRIGGER QUOTES⟩

Nothing is esteemed a miracle, if it ever happens in the common course of nature.
(D. Hume)

If God intervened in the natural order to make a feather land here rather than there for no deep ultimate purpose, or to upset a child's box of toys just for spite, these events would not naturally be described as miracles.
(R. Swinburne)

Specification Link

Consideration of reasons why religious believers accept that miracles occur: evidence from sacred writings, affirmation of faith traditions, personal experience.

The incorrupt body of St Rita who died in 1457, venerated at her shrine in Cascia in Italy. Is it an example of a miracle?

⟨TRIGGER QUOTES⟩

Theology offers you a working arrangement, which leaves the scientist free to continue his experiments and the Christian to continue his prayers. **(C. S. Lewis)**

Omnipotence means power to do all that is intrinsically possible, not to do the intrinsically impossible. You may attribute miracles to Him, but not nonsense. **(C. S. Lewis)**

AO2

What is ... Evaluation and critical analysis ?

The AO2 skills of evaluation and critical analysis mean engaging with the controversies surrounding a subject. This is more than merely describing or listing the points made about a controversy. To achieve this, one weighs up strengths and weaknesses of various sides and takes a position. On the right are three controversies for each issue – you can engage in these by extending their arguments (adding examples, quotes or other details), weighing up their strengths and weaknesses, and coming to a conclusion.

A miraculous escape for some from the sinking of the Titanic. *But if God can save some from the* Titanic, *why can't he save them all?*

❝TRIGGER QUOTES❞

The claim that God has worked a miracle implies that God has singled out certain persons for some benefit which many others do not receive implies that God is unfair. **(J. Keller)**

A miracle is an event described by those to whom it was told by people who did not see it. **(E. Hubbard)**

The question before the human race is, whether the God of nature shall govern the world by his own laws, or whether priests and kings shall rule it by fictitious miracles? **(J. Adams)**

Issue:

The impact of religious experiences upon religious belief and practice

Three evaluative controversies!

- **Controversy 1: *Does a miracle include an intervention by God?***
  Aquinas refers to a divine cause. Similarly, both Hume and Swinburne see intervention by God as a necessary part of the definition, although they also allow for other supernatural agents to be the cause. However, the idea of a contingency miracle implies that the event is **natural** rather than supernatural and is just a beneficial but remarkable coincidence. In classical theism God is seen as **sustainer** as well as creator. For many religious believers, God is seen as always at work in the world. It is just that most times **we don't notice**.

- **Controversy 2: *Doesn't the definition of a miracle point to God being a monster?***
  Many **survivors** from accidents and disasters, etc., have seen their survival against all the odds, as God acting in their lives in a special way. However, by implication, God has also allowed some to perish in the same event. Surely, if God was able to save some, why could he not **save all**? But would that mean that no-one would ever perish? The classical problem of evil issue is why is it that God does not intervene in events such as the **Holocaust** – given he has the power and the motivation of love. But do examples of **God's love outweigh** examples of his apparent inaction?

- **Controversy 3: *Don't the definitions make clear that miracles are impossible?***
  If the definition involves an intervention by God and a breaking of the laws of nature then God would **break his own laws**. Strictly speaking, that is not an impossibility, more an action one would not expect of God. However, can God intervene if he is **outside of time**? Hume states that 'a firm and unalterable experience has established the laws of nature'. This seems to imply that if they are **unalterable** then it is logically impossible for miracles to happen. Hume's definition also implies that no miracle has ever happened in the past since there has been a **uniform experience**, i.e. the laws of nature have always been consistent.

Sp❂tlight: Evaluative judgements

This section contains a special insight that you can use to form a judgement.

Isn't 'sign' a better description of a miracle? Swinburne's definition includes the idea of purpose. He points out that pointless events, that are not consistent with the character of God, cannot be deemed miraculous. The use of the word 'sign' referring to a miracle is found in John's Gospel. It conveys the idea that miracles are pointing to something beyond the actual miracle itself. But can contingency miracles also be signs? It does seem that some people who have a remarkable escape or healing that can be explained by natural causes, still see it as a sign which has an effect on their lives thereafter.

Issue:
How far different definitions of miracles can be considered as contradictory and therefore unsupportive of religious traditions

- **Controversy 1: *Is Swinburne's definition contradictory to Holland's definition?***
  Both Swinburne and Holland focus on the **religious significance** of a miracle. In this area they are very similar. Although it is not clear in Holland's account as to whether God is seen as bringing about the beneficial event by **intervention** (e.g. in the timing so event happens without laws of nature violated), there is one significant difference. For Holland, miracles are **subjective** events – the identifying of a miracle resting solely on the decision of the individual. For Swinburne they are **objective** events – the events are miraculous, whether or not anyone recognises them as such.

- **Controversy 2: *Can the different definitions of miracles be reconciled?***
  Certainly, the definitions have differences, but are they contradictory? In the case of a contingency miracle, a believer, possibly because of **prayer**, might see in the events a divine agency acting – and so describe it as a miracle. The type of event involving violations of laws of nature, are when the divine agency is working at a **different level**. Therefore, perhaps the definitions are merely focusing on **different aspects** and acknowledge two different types of events that can be classed as miracles. On the other hand, **sceptics** would see that both subjective and objective elements in a definition help believers and their religions evade criticism – they can always 'retreat' to the contingency level if there is a lack of evidence.

- **Controversy 3: *Is a violation of a law of nature a contradiction?***
  Laws of nature have **no power** of themselves. They are simply highly generalised shorthand descriptions of how things do in fact happen. In other words, they are the **actual course of events** – the things that we observe. Therefore, to say that they are violated seems inappropriate language. It is rather than the actual course of events on that occasion, is not what we expected. However, if the laws limit what is **possible in reality** then they cannot be broken. Alternatively, the addition of God **changes the circumstances**, such that the law no longer applies because they are now different circumstances. On this understanding – miracles do not violate the laws of nature.

Quick Revision

Consider three miracles and explain how each one could be used to show God is (i) a loving God and (ii) an evil God. Do you think every miracle has this double edge? Explain your view giving reasons. This will help you with an exam question in this area.

❝TRIGGER QUOTES❞

Miracles are coincidences which have a very low probability, but which are, nonetheless, in the realm of probability.
(R. Dawkins)

It is misleading to define a miracle as something that breaks the laws of nature, since the raw material of a miracle is always nature itself, which by definition will behave naturally. It's the cause of the event which is seen to be miraculous.
(C. S. Lewis)

Sp●tlight: Evaluative judgements
This section contains a special insight that you can use to form a judgement.

Is it ever possible to identify an event as a miracle? The development of quantum physics has challenged the mechanistic understanding of the universe in favour of unpredictability. The problem arises because what one thought was a violation of a law of nature might be wrong. So, for example, a sudden remission of cancer may not be a miraculous healing and answer to prayer but a natural event. Perhaps Holland's definition is the only one that identifies a miracle since it rests solely on the decision of the observer.

AO1 Trigger revision activity

 A

ZIP

Definitions of 'miracle'

wonder	transgression of a law of nature	two additions	beneficial coincidences
St Aquinas	divine cause	temporary	toy car
the nature of things	hard sense	point	natural explanations
three kinds of miracles	soft sense	Ray Holland	
David Hume	Richard Swinburne	contingency miracles	
laws of nature			

1 Here is your zip file of portable Triggers. →

2 Practise 'downloading' your zip file of Triggers from memory. See how many you can recall on first attempt. →

3 When you are confident enough, order the Triggers into a list as you may do in an examination situation.

 TIP

Why Trigger?
Remember, your Triggers are to help you transfer your knowledge and understanding in a manageable, efficient and portable manner.

5 Now read through your descriptions and think about ways in which you could develop these using your Trigger quotes. ←

4 Attempt to write one clear sentence to define each Trigger.

 B

ZIP

Why religious believers accept that miracles occur

the reality of God	testimonies	contingency miracles
prayers	veneration	Lourdes
Buddhist texts	divine signature	Christianity
demonic magic	diversity of miracles	authentic

1 Fix the zip file! There are three Triggers missing from this zip file – find them and add them in. →

2 There's another problem: the Triggers are out of order! Put them in the same order as they appear in the AO1 section above. →

3 Practise 'downloading' your zip file of Triggers from memory. See how many you can recall on first attempt.

6 Now read through your definitions and think about ways in which you could develop these using your Trigger quotes. ←

5 Attempt to write one clear sentence to define each Trigger. ←

4 When you are confident enough, order the Triggers into a list as you may do in an examination situation.

AO2 Trigger revision activity

A ZIP

Does a miracle have to include an intervention by God?

Intervention, natural, sustainer, we don't notice	Monster, survivors, save all, Holocaust, God's love outweigh	Impossible, break his own laws, outside of time, unalterable, uniform experience

1 Here is your zip file of portable Triggers. → **2** Practise 'downloading' your zip file of Triggers from memory. See how many you can recall on first attempt. → **3** When you are confident enough, order the Triggers into a list as you may do in an examination situation.

5 Now read through all your sentences and think about ways in which you could develop these using your Trigger quotes, further examples, and noting strengths and weaknesses. ← **4** 'Double-click' each Trigger in your memory – what can you say about an evaluative point of view in a clear sentence? Write this down. Do this for each Trigger in turn. ←

REVISION TIP

Using Trigger quotes
When you choose the Trigger quotes that you wish to use make sure that you explain how they are relevant.

B ZIP

Are the definitions contradictory?

reconciled, sceptics, prayer, different aspects	objective, religious significance, contradictory	actual course of events, changes the circumstances, no power

1 Fix the zip file! There are four Triggers missing from this zip file – find them and add them in. → **2** There's another problem: the Triggers are out of order! Put them in the same order as they appear in the AO2 section above. → **3** Practise 'downloading' your zip file of Triggers from memory. See how many you can recall on first attempt.

6 Now read through all your sentences and think about ways in which you could develop these using your Trigger quotes, further examples, and noting strengths and weaknesses. 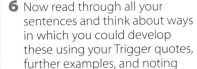 ← **5** Attempt to write one clear sentence to define each Trigger. ← **4** When you are confident enough, order the Triggers into a list as you may do in an examination situation.

Specification Link

David Hume – his scepticism of miracles including challenges relating to testimony-based belief; credibility of witnesses, susceptibility of belief; contradictory nature of faith claims.

AO1

What is ... Knowledge and understanding ?

This is the skill that involves *selecting* the relevant and appropriate information, *organising* it and then *presenting* it through a *personal explanation* that may involve the use of supporting *evidence* and *examples*.

Hume rejected the accounts of the claimed miracles at the Tomb of Abbé Paris despite accepting that the witnesses were of exceptional quality.

Spot the Triggers!

The words in blue are Triggers – key words and phrases that can help you remember knowledge and understanding in this area.

TIP

Theme 3F: Hume and Swinburne on miracles

David Hume's scepticism of miracles

- **Hume's essay** on miracles in *Enquiry Concerning Human Understanding* is often regarded as a major contribution to the debate on miracles.
- His reason for writing it was to make clear that no miracle could be a just **foundation for a religion**. He was particularly referring to Christianity.
- Hume was an **empiricist** and therefore believed that all questions of truth had to be based on experience.
- The essay is in **two parts** and attempts to show that evidence against miracles outweighs evidence for.
- In part one Hume states that a wise man **proportions** his belief to the evidence.

The evidence based on past experience	The persuasiveness of the evidence
Constant experience	Results in full proof
Variable experience	Results in weighing the probability
Consistently and uniformly against (as in case of a miracle)	Concludes that the falsehood of the testimony would have to be more miraculous than the alleged miracle

- Hume defined a miracle as **a violation** of the laws of nature that had been established by a firm and unalterable experience. In order to identify a miracle, there must be a uniform experience against such an event.
- In part two of his essay, Hume examines the **quality of testimony** required:

The quality of testimony required	Hume's conclusion
Educated, trustworthy, not deluded; have a lot to lose if found lying	None found in **sufficient number**
Not swayed by emotion; no **vested interest** or bias; must not be religionists who promote known false miracles	People look for marvels and wonders, and tend to believe
Miracle stories not from **ignorant people** or from remote countries	Stories acquired authority without critical or rational inquiry

- Hume raised a further challenge against miracles: evidence for a miracle is **contradicted** by other evidence for a miracle from a different religious tradition. They are self-cancelling.
- For instance, a miracle in Hinduism would **discredit the truth claim** of Islam and vice versa.

Richard Swinburne's defence of miracles

- Swinburne's main writing on miracles is in his book The *Concept of Miracle*.
- He accepts Hume's **three arguments** about credibility of witnesses but rejects the high standard that Hume demands. For instance, just how many is a 'sufficient number'?
- Swinburne also rejects the assumption that all believers are either deceivers or **deceived**.
- He accuses Hume of assuming that ignorant nations are by definition those who believe miracles happen.

- Swinburne then examines the issue of **conflicting testimony**:

Swinburne's principles for weighing conflicting testimony	Example
Different types of testimony need to be weighted differently	My own memory ought to count more than testimony of another
Different testimonies need to be weighted according to their reliability	Witness shown unreliable in previous testimonies
Multiple similar testimony is stronger than a lesser number of contrary testimonies	Five people saying same thing stronger than two saying something contrary

- He argues that there can be evidence that a law of nature has been **violated**.
- He uses the phrase '**non-repeatable counter-instance**' so that it is clear that the 'miracle' is not just a modified law of nature, but an exception to the ordinary course of nature.
- Hume had claimed that singular past events could not be examined directly, but Swinburne points to the character, mind and competence of the original witnesses; **physical traces** of event and present effects resulting from event.
- In addition, if there is other evidence for God/Divine Being, the event is **consistent** with that Being's character.
- If there is no other explanation – then Swinburne argues it is **reasonable to believe** that God/Divine Being caused the event.
- If an event is normally caused by a human being but the event then happens without human beings, Swinburne argues that it would be justifiable to claim a **non-material being** caused it – i.e. a god.
- He claims that most alleged miracles neither give rise to conflict nor are **incompatible** with each other.
- Miracles show **power** of God rather than being concerned with doctrine.

Specification Link

Richard Swinburne – his defence of miracles, including definitions of natural laws and contradictions of Hume's arguments regarding contradictory nature of faith claims and credibility of witnesses.

Joseph Smith brings a corpse back to life. Would Hume be convinced by this claimed miracle?

Quick Revision

In your own words, explain the three areas that Hume raised about the quality of testimony that was required to believe a miracle had occurred. Do you think his requirements are reasonable? Give your reasons. What quality of testimony do you think is required to believe a miracle has occurred? Explain why you have chosen this quality. This activity will help you with an exam question on Hume's arguments about quality of testimony.

'TRIGGER QUOTES'

There are no logical difficulties in supposing that there could be strong historical evidence for the occurrence of miracles. Whether there is such evidence is, of course, another matter. **(R. Swinburne)**

'Uniform experience' Hume writes (for example, that dead men do not come back to life), amounts to a proof, as if the 'laws' were regulatory, not descriptive, in a closed or self-contained universe. **(A. Thiselton)**

… no testimony is sufficient to establish a miracle, unless the testimony be of such a kind, that its falsehood would be more miraculous, than the fact, which it endeavours to establish. **(D. Hume)**

Inquiry is fatal to certainty. **(W. Durant)**

AO2

What is ... Evaluation and critical analysis **?**

The AO2 skills of evaluation and critical analysis mean engaging with the controversies surrounding a subject. This is more than merely describing or listing the points made about a controversy. To achieve this, one weighs up strengths and weaknesses of various sides and takes a position. On the right are three controversies for each issue – you can engage in these by extending their arguments (adding examples, quotes or other details), weighing up their strengths and weaknesses, and coming to a conclusion.

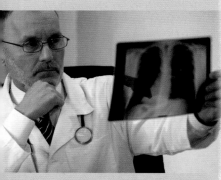

Are there any tests that would prove a miracle?

❛TRIGGER QUOTES❜

It is not to science, therefore but to metaphysics, imaginative literature or religion that we must turn for answers to questions having to do with first and last things.   **(P. Medawar)**

... laws of nature are only intended to describe events within the natural realm and miracles are outside the natural realm.
(T. Drange)

Issue:
The effectiveness of the challenges to belief in miracles

Three evaluative controversies!

☐ **Controversy 1: *Is the reliability of testimony the problem with believing in miracles?***

It seems that Hume was quite **sceptical** about the credibility of testimony and took a view of guilty until proven innocent, whilst Swinburne seems to be more **trusting** and assumes testimony is probably reliable until proven otherwise. But is either of them free from bias? Most conclude that Hume did not believe in God, whilst Swinburne does believe in God. Perhaps **the real difficulty** is to set aside our prejudices and set beliefs so they do not colour our assessment of the evidence. For many, a belief or a disbelief in miracles, would require a **paradigm shift** – a radical change in world view. It would mean discarding the ideas and beliefs that had been the basis of their entire way of thinking.

☐ **Controversy 2: *Does Hume use an a priori argument?***

If Hume is an empiricist then surely knowledge comes from **experience** and so he cannot have a priori arguments. However, some scholars argue that Hume presents an a priori argument in **part one** of his essay when he says that laws of nature are unalterably uniform. Perhaps the problem is the use of the word 'argument'. Hume was engaged in reasoning and there is a **difference** between an argument which is a priori, inductive (which Hume would not accept as an empiricist) and arguments that have elements of **deductive reasoning**. Therefore, Hume could be interpreted as being consistent with his empiricist view and only using deductive reasoning rather than deductive arguments.

☐ **Controversy 3: *Do miracles invalidate science?***

If miracles are events that break the laws of nature, then it suggests that science, which established these laws, is **unreliable** and not an accurate predictor of future events. Indeed, 'science' is not some **entity** that can rule with authority what must or must not happen. It merely describes what it expected to happen on the basis of what has happened in the past. Science itself is **neutral**. However, it is quite rational to believe that a miracle has occurred while allowing the possibility that evidence will later be found that it was not a miracle.

Sp⬤tlight: **Evaluative judgements**
This section contains a special insight that you can use to form a judgement.

Did Hume think miracles were impossible? Even when confronted with credible witnesses of number, integrity and education to the alleged miracles at the Tomb of Abbé Paris, Hume dismissed them as irrelevant on the grounds that the miraculous nature of the event was sufficient to reject it. Many also interpret his definition as denying the possibility of miracles since he referred to a 'firm and unalterable experience' that established the laws of nature, i.e. the laws had never been, and could never be, broken.

Issue:

The extent to which Swinburne's responses to Hume can be accepted as valid

- **Controversy 1: *Aren't miracles conflicting if they occur in different religious traditions?***

  Hume argued that the **truth claims** of a religion were demonstrated by miracles within that religion. Therefore, if miracles occurred in more than one religion, they cancelled out each other. Swinburne argues that miracles in different religions have not been about truth claims but about demonstrations of the power of God. He does not see them as **contests** between different religions but about the existence of a God. But what about Christianity? The New Testament itself states that the resurrection of Jesus is **proof** that Christianity is the only true faith. Some argue that God reveals himself in **different ways** to different people through different religions.

- **Controversy 2: *Is multiple testimony reasonable to demand?***

  It might seem that more people who claim they witnessed an event is **more persuasive** than one person's claim to witness it. However, is the quantity of witnesses the deciding factor? Does it not depend more on the **quality** of the witnesses? Hume seems right to demand witnesses that were educated, trustworthy, able to avoid being deluded, and have a lot to risk if they were found lying. But can miracles only take place in such public circumstances? Often miracles are claimed to be answers to prayer – events that are often more **private**.

- **Controversy 3: *Isn't the idea of 'purpose' the important element of a miracle?***

  Swinburne included the idea of purpose as an element of his definition of a miracle. Miracles were not just odd happenings but events that had a clear divine purpose – that were reflective of **God's nature and character**. However, Hume also saw purpose in miracles. Indeed, he states that his reason for writing his essay on miracles was to **invalidate** the Christian Faith, since he saw it rested on its claim of miracles to be the one true religion. But surely the fact that they are contrary to normal events and break the laws of nature is the important element. Without that, the events would not be seen as the work of a God. However, don't Holland's **contingency miracles** function within the natural laws and still have purpose?

Sp●tlight: Evaluative judgements

This section contains a special insight that you can use to form a judgement.

Is testimony the only source of evidence? Certainly, Hume focuses on testimony since he sees miracles as single past events and so they cannot be examined other than by those who witnessed them at the time. However, Swinburne maintains that miracles are open to other forms of evidence. For instance, physical effects can be seen, such as a healed withered hand or by before and after X-rays.

TIP

Remember, your triggers are to help you transfer your knowledge and understanding in a manageable, efficient and portable manner.

Quick Revision

In your own words, explain how Swinburne responds to the problem of conflicting testimony. Make a list of the strengths of his argument and a list of the weaknesses. Do you think Swinburne successfully answers Hume's concerns about conflicting testimony? Give reasons to justify your view. This activity will help you with an exam question on Swinburne's response to Hume.

❝TRIGGER QUOTES❞

What Jesus did here in Cana of Galilee was the first of the signs through which he revealed his glory and his disciples believed in him.   **(John 2:11 NIV)**

Science deals with but a partial aspect of reality; there is not the slightest reason for supposing that everything science ignores is less real than what it accepts.
(J. Sullivan)

AO1 Trigger revision activity

A

ZIP

David Hume's scepticism of miracles

vested interest	a violation	variable	Hume's essay
discredit the truth claim	constant	foundation for a religion	proportions
two parts	ignorant people	consistently and uniformly against	
	quality of testimony		

1 Fix the zip file! There are three Triggers missing from this zip file – find them and add them in.

2 There's another problem: the Triggers are out of order! Put them in the same order as they appear in the AO1 section above.

3 Practise 'downloading' your zip file of Triggers from memory. See how many you can recall on first attempt.

6 Now read through your definitions and think about ways in which you could develop these using your Trigger quotes.

5 Attempt to write one clear sentence to define each Trigger.

4 When you are confident enough, order the Triggers into a list as you may do in an examination situation.

B

ZIP

Richard Swinburne's defence of miracles

1 There are no Triggers in this zip file! Find and add in the relevant Triggers.

2 Now put the Triggers in the same order as they appear in the AO1 section above.

3 Practise 'downloading' your zip file of Triggers from memory. See how many you can recall on first attempt.

6 Now read through your definitions and think about ways in which you could develop these using your Trigger quotes.

5 Attempt to write one clear sentence to define each Trigger.

4 When you are confident enough, order the Triggers into a list as you may do in an examination situation.

AO2 Trigger revision activity

A

ZIP

Is belief in miracles reasonable?

difference, part one, a priori argument, deductive reasoning

the real difficulty, sceptical, trusting

entity, unreliable, invalidate science

1 Fix the zip file! There are three Triggers missing from this zip file – find them and add them in.

2 There's another problem: the Triggers are out of order! Put them in the same order as they appear in the AO2 section above.

3 Practise 'downloading' your zip file of Triggers from memory. See how many you can recall on first attempt.

6 Now read through all your sentences and think about ways in which you could develop these using your Trigger quotes, further examples, and noting strengths and weaknesses.

5 Attempt to write one clear sentence to define each Trigger.

4 When you are confident enough, order the Triggers into a list as you may do in an examination situation.

B

ZIP

Are Swinburne's responses to Hume convincing?

1 There are no Triggers in this zip file! Find and add in the relevant Triggers.

2 Now put the Triggers in the same order as they appear in the AO2 section above.

3 Practise 'downloading' your zip file of Triggers from memory. See how many you can recall on first attempt.

6 Now read through all your sentences and think about ways in which you could develop these using your Trigger quotes, further examples, and noting strengths and weaknesses.

5 Attempt to write one clear sentence to define each Trigger.

4 When you are confident enough, order the Triggers into a list as you may do in an examination situation.

Religious language

AO1

What is ...
Knowledge and
understanding

This is the skill that involves *selecting* the relevant and appropriate information, *organising* it and then *presenting* it through a *personal explanation* that may involve the use of supporting *evidence* and *examples*.

Spot the Triggers!
The words in blue are Triggers – key words and phrases that can help you remember knowledge and understanding in this area.

TIP

TRIGGER QUOTES

If one says that God is very different from anything else, can one really talk significantly about him at all? **(B. Davies)**

For to say that 'God exists' is to make a metaphysical utterance which cannot be either true or false. **(A. J. Ayer)**

Theme 4A: **Inherent problems of religious language**

Difficulties with religious language

An intelligible conversation is possible about a brick house because we share a common experience. Not all people, however, have a shared experience of the love of God. Some find this to be an unintelligible claim.

- We use language to communicate **experiences** we have had.
- The success of communication depends on the degree to which we share a **common base** of experiences.
- For instance, if we are speaking about a '**brick house**', my communication will be intelligible if those listening have experienced a 'brick house'. If they have not, it will take much more work to ensure the intelligibility of our speech.
- When our communication is concerned with the world of **sense experience**, there is usually a common experience of understanding and meaning.
- When religious language merely attempts to **describe religious buildings**, the classification of religious texts or the posture of prayer, this language is intelligible because it is concerned with the world of sense experience.
- But sometimes our communication is concerned with the **metaphysical**, that which is 'beyond' (meta) the physical world.
- Much religious language is metaphysical: statements about the nature of the divine world, the attributes of God, the state of one's **soul**, etc.
- Many statements about ideas, emotions, ethics and aesthetics can also be seen as 'metaphysical'.
- It is much more difficult to reach a consensus of meaning about a metaphysical statement ('**God is love**') than about an experience of the senses ('There is a brick house on 5th Avenue').
- **Logical positivists** said that language (other than purely logical formulations) is only meaningful if it can be verified by empirical means.
- When religious believers describe the 'Ultimate' or 'God' as 'infinite' or 'timeless', they are not able to appeal to a common set of experiences with those who are not religious adherents – those who believe that the only experiences that exist are 'in' time and space.
- Religious language is made more difficult by the fact that religious

believers **cannot agree** between themselves on the meaning of metaphysical language.

- ☐ **David Hume** has said that statements which did not contain abstract mathematical reasoning or insights about facts and existence based on evidence were nothing more than 'sophistry and illusion'.
- ☐ Different words for the divine (God/The Ultimate/Allah/Brahman/ Dharmakaya, etc.) are associated with concepts that differ between religions, making religious statements difficult to understand and reconcile.
- ☐ A further difficulty is that 'religions of the Book' (Christianity, Judaism and Islam) use words to declare truths about a God whom they believe to be beyond words – how is this possible?
- ☐ Some theologians believe that there is **nothing** that can be said about God because God is not a 'thing' in our universe.

Two types of language

Cognitive language	Non-cognitive language
Is about the external and **physical world** – it relates to objects and fact.	Is **outside** of that which can be empirically proven, such as statements about ethics, aesthetics and religion.
Can be judged as **true or false** because it can be examined by empirical means.	Cannot be judged as true or false because it **cannot be examined** by empirical means.
Involves acts of **cognition** – coming to knowledge through our experience of the five senses (taste, touch, hearing, sight and smell).	Involves acts of **intuition** and/or the claim that knowledge has arisen from a source outside of the five senses.
Can be **verified**, proved true, by using empirical evidence.	Is **unverifiable** because it cannot be examined through the five senses.
Is **falsifiable**, that is, it uses statements which can be questioned and proven false if there is evidence.	Is **not falsifiable** – statements cannot be proven either true or false.

- ☐ Religious believers may see their claims (i.e. 'There is a God') cognitively – as claims that can be proven true or false through empirical means.
- ☐ Examples of cognitive approaches to religious language include arguments for God which make use of empirical evidence such as the **cosmological** or teleological/design arguments.
- ☐ These believers see that their statements **correspond** to their experiences in the empirical world.
- ☐ An example of a cognitive approach to religious language is the claim that the intricacy and beauty of the world cannot be explained through evolution alone. This statement **may be debated** and tested through empirical evidence.
- ☐ Other religious believers may see their claims as non-cognitive – as statements which cannot be proven true or false through empirical means.
- ☐ These believers see that their statements have **coherent perspective** which expresses their convictions about the nature of reality.
- ☐ An example of a non-cognitive claim is the assertion by Pascal that we have an existential emptiness that only God can satisfy. This statement cannot be established by **empirical means**.

'TRIGGER QUOTES'

When we assert what we take to be a fact (or deny what is alleged to be a fact), we are using language cognitively. **(J. Hick)**

... this infinite abyss can be filled only with an infinite and immutable object; in other words by God himself. **(B. Pascal)**

We do not ask of a swearword, or a command, or the baptismal formula whether it is true. **(J. Hick)**

Specification Link

The differences between cognitive and non-cognitive language.

Religious language can be a coherent viewpoint or perspective through which we look at the world. As such, it is non-cognitive but meaningful.

Quick Revision

Create 10 statements which have nothing to do with religion – make 5 of these cognitive statements (i.e. based on sensory experience) and 5 non-cognitive, which fall outside of sensory experience. Then, make a new list of 10 cognitive and non-cognitive statements about religion. This will help you with an exam question which requires an explanation of religious language.

AO2

What is ... Evaluation and critical analysis **?**

The AO2 skills of evaluation and critical analysis mean engaging with the controversies surrounding a subject. This is more than merely describing or listing the points made about a controversy. To achieve this, one weighs up strengths and weaknesses of various sides and takes a position. On the right are three controversies for each issue – you can engage in these by extending their arguments (adding examples, quotes or other details), weighing up their strengths and weaknesses, and coming to a conclusion.

If God is utterly transcendent and therefore beyond words, is it not a contradiction to claim that there is a book which reveals truth about God?

❝ TRIGGER QUOTES ❞

Genesis (1:2 6) says: 'Let us make man to our image and likeness.' Therefore, some likeness exists between God and creature. **(T. Aquinas)**

Our environment is thus religiously ambiguous. **(J. Hick)**

The experience that would verify Christian belief in God is the experience of participating in that eventual fulfilment. **(J. Hick)**

... without a blik there can be no explanation; for it is by our bliks that we decide what is and what is not an explanation. **(R. Hare)**

Issue:

The solutions presented by religious philosophers for the inherent problems of using religious language

Three evaluative controversies!

- **Controversy 1:** *Experience can be extended by* *analogy*.
  The claims of religions are, literally, '**non-sense**' to those who do not share a base experience with religious believers. Yet, analogies enable us to communicate meaningfully when we do not have a shared **base of experience**. An analogy is, of course, when we speak of one thing in terms of something else. Aquinas said, for example, that if we can understand what a 'good' human being is, then we can begin to comprehend (though never fully comprehend) an infinitely good God. This recognises that language has limits but it also opens up the **possibility** for communication on religious themes.

- **Controversy 2:** *Religious language can be* *eschatologically verified*.
  The **logical positivists** insisted that that the only meaningful propositions are those which are either logically necessary definitions ('all eye doctors are oculists') or can be verified by an appeal to the senses. Many religious believers, such as John Hick, view their faith as real, corresponding to the **objective world** – but that the evidence for this will only be fully known at the eschaton (the end of time). In the meantime, we must employ **faith** in the face of ambiguous evidence. This is called 'eschatological verification'.

- **Controversy 3:** *Religious language is meaningful because it is* *coherent*.
  One criticism of religious language is that it does not correspond to the 'real world' of what can be proven thought the senses. Yet, do we not believe in many things that cannot be proven by the senses: love, moral beliefs, the 'fact' that some things are 'beautiful' or 'ugly'? Religious language is meaningful because it **expresses a perspective** or attitude on life that provides a coherent way of looking at the world, prior to our knowledge gained by sense experience. This can be compared to wearing a set of **lenses** through which life becomes meaningful. The philosopher Richard Hare gives this idea the name, '**blik**' – an unfalsifiable conviction which leads to a meaningful world view.

Sp❖tlight: Evaluative judgements

This section contains a special insight that you can use to form a judgement.

Can it make sense to both speak about God and say that God is beyond speech? The Abrahamic religions (Christianity, Islam and Judaism) describe God using a variety of attributes: infinite, omnipotent, omniscient, etc. Yet, these same religions declare God to be transcendent and beyond human understanding: 'Can you find out the deep things of God? Can you find out the limit of the Almighty?' (Job 11:7).

Issue:

The exclusive context of religious belief for an understanding of religious language

- **Controversy 1:** *Language is based on unique and exclusive rules.* **Ludwig Wittgenstein** taught that we learn language only through specific communities who have their own rules for expression. He used the concept of a '**game**' to reinforce the idea that each word and phrase we use is guided by certain rules, which one can only fully learn by participating in the 'games' of a community. Just as we would not expect to play the game of cricket by using the rules of backgammon, we cannot expect to understand the language of Islam if we have been raised as a Zen Buddhist. However, Wittgenstein did not say that we couldn't understand religious language – just that it would take an enormous **commitment** to do so.

- **Controversy 2:** *The fact of religious conversions prove that religious language is understood outside of its specific context.* Every year there are conversions to all of the main world religions. For instance, it is quite popular for those disenchanted with Christianity to become Buddhists. **Sinead O'Connor** converted from Christianity to Islam. This means that the language of specific religions has reached **beyond its context**. However, it could be argued that those who convert never fully understand the religion to which they convert, or that they may **already know** the religion to which they are converting. For instance, C. S. Lewis had a 'Christian' upbringing and converted to the Church which he already knew intimately.

- **Controversy 3:** *Religious language is related to the objective world.* Richard Swinburne argues that religious statements are 'realist' and should be regarded as scientific hypotheses; he appeals to the vast number of religious experiences and **arguments for God**. John Hick believed that the differences in beliefs between religions can be accounted for by the fact that they share a '**common core**', which is interpreted though culture, history, language, geography, etc. However, the fact that many do not recognise the scientific nature of religious statements nor the supposed 'common core' is grounds to doubt these ideas. As there are no proofs for religious claims that would satisfy a **logical positivist**, we must conclude that religious language is not understood beyond religious contexts.

TIP

If you decide to use a Trigger quote in an exam response, always take time to briefly explain what the quote means and how it fits into your argument.

Quick Revision

Find three phrases that specific religious believers might use in the religion you are studying (e.g. 'Our Father who art in heaven ...' [Christianity] or 'Hare Krishna' [Hinduism], etc.). Now, make a case of why these three phrases are incomprehensible and meaningless to those outside of the religion AND make a case of how they could be seen to be meaningful. This will help you with an examination evaluation question on religious language.

❛TRIGGER QUOTES❜

One does not have to know exactly what a word means in order to have some understanding of it   (**B. Davies**)

... the meaning of a word is its use in the language.   (**L. Wittgenstein**)

Sp◉tlight: **Evaluative judgements**

This section contains a special insight that you can use to form a judgement.

It is possible to view religious language as non-cognitive (that is, not able to be judged as true nor false) and see that its meaning can be understood outside of its particular contexts. R. B. Braithwaite viewed religious language as a way of stating ethical convictions. For example, asserting that 'God is love' is a way of announcing one's intention to follow a loving way of life. It is possible for two religions to have (and recognise in each other) the same policy for living – they just use different stories to illustrate their moral intention.

AO1 Trigger revision activity

A ZIP

Difficulties with religious language

1 There are no Triggers in this zip file! Find and add in the relevant Triggers.

2 Now put the Triggers in the same order as they appear in the AO1 section above.

3 Practise 'downloading' your zip file of Triggers from memory. See how many you can recall on first attempt.

6 Now read through your definitions and think about ways in which you could develop these using your Trigger quotes.

5 Attempt to write one clear sentence to define each Trigger.

4 When you are confident enough, order the Triggers into a list as you may do in an examination situation.

B ZIP

Two types of language

coruscant	intuition
empirical means	non-falsifiable
	cosmological
cognition	correspond
verified	feud
falsifiable	outside
electrostaff	muddled
unverifiable	true or false

1 Find the unhelpful Triggers! **This zip file contains several inappropriate or irrelevant Triggers**. Find these and replace them with the real Triggers from the AO1 section.

2 There's another problem: the Triggers are out of order! Put them in the same order as they appear in the AO1 section above.

3 Practise 'downloading' your zip file of Triggers from memory. See how many you can recall on first attempt.

6 Now read through your definitions and think about ways in which you could develop these using your Trigger quotes.

5 Attempt to write one clear sentence to define each Trigger.

4 When you are confident enough, order the Triggers into a list as you may do in an examination situation.

AO2 Trigger revision activity

A

ZIP

Solutions for the problem of religious language

1 There are no Triggers in this zip file! Find and add in the relevant Triggers.

2 Now put the Triggers in the same order as they appear in the AO2 section above.

3 Practise 'downloading' your zip file of Triggers from memory. See how many you can recall on first attempt.

4 When you are confident enough, order the Triggers into a list as you may do in an examination situation.

5 Attempt to write one clear sentence to define each Trigger.

6 Now read through all your sentences and think about ways in which you could develop these using your Trigger quotes, further examples, and noting strengths and weaknesses.

B

ZIP

Religious language as exclusive to context

Objective world, arguments for God, common core, political lobbyist	**Religious conversions, Sinead O'Connor, hyperspace, already know**	**Exclusive rules, Ludwig Beethoven, monopoly, commitment**

1 Find the unhelpful Triggers! **This zip file contains several inappropriate or irrelevant Triggers**. Find these and replace them with the real Triggers from the AO2 section.

2 There's another problem: the Triggers are out of order! Put them in the same order as they appear in the AO2 section above.

3 Practise 'downloading' your zip file of Triggers from memory. See how many you can recall on first attempt.

4 When you are confident enough, order the Triggers into a list as you may do in an examination situation.

5 Attempt to write one clear sentence to define each Trigger.

6 Now read through all your sentences and think about ways in which you could develop these using your Trigger quotes, further examples, and noting strengths and weaknesses.

Theme 4B: Religious language as cognitive, but meaningless

Logical positivism

Specification Link

Logical positivism – (A. J. Ayer).

Spot the Triggers!
The words in blue are Triggers – key words and phrases that can help you remember knowledge and understanding in this area.

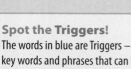

AO1

What is ... Knowledge and understanding?

This is the skill that involves *selecting* the relevant and appropriate information, *organising* it and then *presenting* it through a *personal explanation* that may involve the use of supporting *evidence* and *examples*.

Ensure you achieve a solid foundation for your knowledge on the tenets of logical positivism. This area emerges throughout the entire religious language theme.

The truth of a synthetic proposition is established by observation and experience.

- The logical positivists (aka the '**Vienna circle**') were a group of scientists and philosophers from Austria and Germany who met during the 1920s.
- This group supported a **scientific world view** in line with empirical methods by insisting on precision with the language we use to describe the world.
- Their focus was on the **reduction** of all knowledge to basic scientific and logical formulations.
- This group maintained that there are only **two forms** of discourse that could be considered meaningful: (i) knowledge gained by logical reasoning (analytic statements) and (ii) statements open to empirical evidence (synthetic statements).
- **A. J. Ayer** popularised logical positivism in his book, *Language, Truth and Logic*; in it, he explains the relationship of analytic and synthetic statements to the wide range of language we use.
- An **analytic statement** is a priori (based on theoretical deduction) and determined by the meaning of the terms; one does not need empirical observation to establish its truth.
- Analytic statements are meaningful because of **logical conditions**; these types of statements include mathematical statements and tautologies.
- **Mathematical equations** are empty of factual content; rather, they spell out relations between symbols ($1 + 1 = 2$).
- **Tautologies** are abstract statements which are necessarily true because of a formal logical structure ('a rose is a rose').
- The other form of meaningful statement are those which are open to empirical evidence; these are known as **synthetic statements**.
- Synthetic statements are a posteriori (based on **observation** and experience) and related to objective reality ('there is a tree on the hill').
- Ayer sums this up: 'A proposition is analytic when its **validity** depends solely on the definitions of the symbols it contains, and synthetic when its validity is determined by the facts of experience.'

Verification and meaningless statements

- The **verification principle** is the doctrine that a statement is only meaningful if it is empirically verifiable or else tautological.
- The logical positivists maintained that all other statements, falling outside of logical reasoning and **empirical evidence**, were held to be meaningless.
- **Metaphysical** (literally, 'beyond the physical') statements are those which claim to speak about a reality beyond the empirical world.
- Whereas earlier scientific criticisms accused metaphysics as unscientific, logical positivists extended this criticism to declare them **meaningless**.
- 'Meaningless' is the same as saying that these statements are neither true nor false – they are wholly **empty** of any significance.
- Included in this critique is not only **religion**, but statements about morality, idealistic philosophy and aesthetics.
- Examples of **meaningless statements** include: 'there is a God', 'the primary basis of the world is the unconscious' and 'the world is beautiful'; these are not logically necessary propositions, nor can they be verified by empirical means.
- Ayer viewed all statements of aesthetics, ethics and religion as unverifiable and viewed these fields of study as 'devoted to the production of **nonsense**'.
- Ayer **developed logical positivism** by establishing the difference between verifiability in principle and verifiability in practice.
- A proposition is **verifiable in principle** if one is unable to make actual observations but knows the kind of observations that would make the difference between truth and falsehood.
- For example, in Ayer's day the proposition, 'there are mountains on the other side of the moon' was not practically verifiable. Yet, it would be verifiable in principle.
- Ayer also introduced the notion of **weak and strong verification**. Strong verification maintains that the truth of a proposition can be conclusively established in experience.
- Weak verification means that it is possible for experience to make a proposition probable.
- For example, the statement of a **general law** such as 'all humans are mortal' defies 'strong verification' because we cannot conclude this in each case – as we would have to be present at every death! However, it is true in a weak sense because there are many observations that support its truth.
- These developments do not change Ayer's view that metaphysical claims are nonsense, because we do not know what evidence would even count in their favour – even in the weak sense.

❛TRIGGER QUOTES❜

... a sentence [has] literal meaning if and only if the proposition it expressed was either analytic or empirically verifiable.
(A. J. Ayer)

... it is only by the occurrence of some sense-content ... that any statement about a material thing is actually verified ...
(A. J. Ayer)

... no sentence which purports to describe the nature of a transcendent god can possess any literal significance.
(A. J. Ayer)

Ayer recognised that any claim to know a past event, such as a historic battle, could not be verified in the strong sense because we cannot have direct experience of that event. However, it should be considered verifiable in the weak sense if there is evidence to show that its occurrence was probable.

Falsification

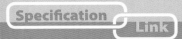

Falsification – nothing can counter the belief (Antony Flew).

- **Falsification** refers to the view that science is not, essentially, about verification but falsification.
- Science proceeds without verification; what is required are statements that can be falsified – one knows how they could be disproved. If a statement is non-falsifiable, it is **meaningless**.
- In other words, science moves from **theory to observation** and not the other way around. E.g., 'objects on the earth are subject to gravity' is a falsifiable statement because we know what it would take to disprove it (i.e. levitating objects).
- Anthony Flew argued that the **religious assertion** 'a loving God exists' is a falsifiable statement if we accept that it could be disproved (i.e. if there were horrendous and pointless suffering in the world).
- However, religious believers **qualify** their assertions to such a degree that they are no longer falsifiable statements (i.e. they declare, 'God's love is an unworldly and inscrutable love').
- Religious believers are guilty of qualifying their assertions to such a degree so as to render them **non-falsifiable** and therefore meaningless.
- Flew uses John **Wisdom's parable** of the clearing to illustrate this: two explorers come upon a clearing and one argues that there is a gardener who tends the clearing – yet there is no definite evidence that this is the case. The 'believer' then qualifies the type of gardener to which he is referring: 'he' is an invisible, intangible gardener. These qualifications make his assertion non-falsifiable and therefore meaningless.

TRIGGER QUOTES

Now to assert that such and such is the case is necessarily equivalent to denying that such and such is not the case. **(A. Flew)**

... if there is nothing which a putative assertion denies then there is nothing which it asserts either ... **(A. Flew)**

What would have to occur or to have occurred to constitute for you a disproof of the love of, or the existence of God? **(A. Flew)**

Flew's interaction with theology	
The argument	**Explanation**
1. The believer says, 'God loves us as a father loves his children.'	This is an assertion. Something must be able to **'count' against** this for it to be considered a falsifiable statement.
2. The sceptic replies, 'A child dies of inoperable throat cancer. Where is God's love?'	This is **evidence** that counts against the assertion above.
3. The believer says, 'God's love is really beyond human understanding.'	Instead of responding to point 2, the believer has withdrawn the original assertion and replaced it with something that resembles it, but is a **tautology**.
4. The sceptic says, 'You've **changed the assertion** into something that cannot be proved or disproved.'	The sceptic is accusing the believer of making a non-falsifiable (and therefore meaningless) assertion.

Be prepared to explain the difference between the principle of verification and the principle of falsification.

Flew believed that human suffering counts against an assertion of the love of God for humanity.

Criticisms of verification and falsification

- The principle of verification is **not itself verifiable**.
- For, the principle of verification is **not an empirical**/synthetic proposition, therefore according to its own criteria it must be either meaningless or a tautology.
- If the principle of verification is a tautology, then it is an **arbitrary** definition of meaningfulness.
- Ayer's development of the principle to include a weak form in order to handle historical statements and general laws of science demonstrates the **deficiency** of the principle.
- The verification principle can be used by religious believers, such as John Hick, to argue for the meaningfulness of belief in God based on '**eschatological verification**' – (i.e. that belief can be verified after death).
- R. M. Hare said that meaningfulness for believers does not come from falsifiable statements but from the **overall perspective** or attitude which belief provides.
- Hare coined the term '**blik**' to describe the way we have of looking at our lives and experiences.

A 'blik' is an overall perspective through which we see the world. For Hare, observations cannot prove or disprove a blik; it exists prior to observation.

- Bliks **precede observation** and provide a coherent view of life; all of us have bliks.
- Basil Mitchell agreed with Flew on the importance of falsifiability but disagreed that believers always qualify their beliefs into a state of meaninglessness.
- The fact of suffering does indeed count against religious belief – but it does not count decisively against it because the case against religious belief is ambiguous. **Faith** is the deciding factor.
- Mitchell tells the **parable of the stranger** who claims to be working with the resistance, though also fraternises with the enemy. There is evidence to both support and doubt the stranger's claim; it is legitimate also to have faith in that claim.
- Richard **Swinburne** notes that language can be meaningful even without empirical evidence to support it.
- Swinburne uses the illustration of **toys** that come to life at times when people are not able to detect them. There is no way that the claim can be falsified. Yet, it is a claim many would find meaningful.
- This presents a challenge to the weak verification principle because we **cannot use observation** to confirm or disconfirm this report.

Specification Link

Criticisms of verification: the verification principle cannot itself be verified; neither can historical events; universal scientific statements; the concept of eschatological verification goes against this. Criticisms of falsification: Richard Hare –bliks (the way that a person views the world gives meaning to them even if others do not share the same view); Basil Mitchell – partisan and the stranger (certain things can be meaningful even when they cannot be falsified); Swinburne – toys in the cupboard (concept meaningful even though falsifying the statement is not possible).

Quick Revision

Write down the different reasons why Ayer and Flew would not accept as meaningful the assertion 'a loving God exists'. Ensure you note the differences between how this statement can be seen to fail both the verification principle and the falsification principle. This will help you with an AO1 examination question asking for an explanation of these approaches.

❛TRIGGER QUOTES❜

... differences between bliks about the world cannot be settled by observation of what happens in the world. **(R. M. Hare)**

The theologian would surely not deny that the fact of pain counts against the assertion that God loves men. **(B. Mitchell)**

... I agree with Flew that theological utterances must be assertions. **(B. Mitchell)**

... there are plenty of examples of statements which some people judge to be factual which are not apparently confirmable or disconfirmable through observation. **(R. Swinburne)**

AO2

What is ...
Evaluation and
critical analysis ■ **?**

The AO2 skills of evaluation and critical analysis mean engaging with the controversies surrounding a subject. This is more than merely describing or listing the points made about a controversy. To achieve this, one weighs up strengths and weaknesses of various sides and takes a position. On the right are three controversies for each issue – you can engage in these by extending their arguments (adding examples, quotes or other details), weighing up their strengths and weaknesses, and coming to a conclusion.

John Hick says that the assertions of religious believers are verifiable – but not presently because the evidence appears ambiguous. At the end of the journey, in the afterlife, we will know with certainty that religious points of view have made sense. Hick calls this 'eschatological verification'.

❛TRIGGER QUOTES❜

If 'god' is a metaphysical term, then it cannot be even probable that a god exists.
(A. J. Ayer)

And yet when they turn the last corner [to the 'Celestial city'] it will be apparent that one of them has been right all the time and the other wrong. **(J. Hick)**

[the clearing parable:] The Believer's earlier statement had been so eroded by qualification that it was no assertion at all. **(B. Mitchell).**

Issue:
The persuasiveness of arguments asserting either the meaningfulness or meaninglessness of religious language

Three evaluative controversies!

☐ **Controversy 1:** *A single bird with wings is worth more than 1,000 winged angels!*
Scientific discoveries which benefit all of our lives are founded on the ability to **verify** propositions in the objective, observable world – or at least to propose theories which we know could be falsified were certain conditions to be met. Just compare the assertion 'a bird has wings' to 'an angel has wings'. The former can be established though **observation**; the latter is not verifiable through an appeal to observable phenomena. Some religious believers, however, might argue that we believe in very important things which cannot be proven such as '**love**', 'beauty' and moral laws.

☐ **Controversy 2:** *Logical positivists miss the point: religious language is* **non-cognitive.**
Richard Hare noted that all humans have an **overall perspective** or attitude which shapes the observations they make. He called this a 'blik'. Bliks are even more real to us than facts. Therefore, we should see religious statements as perspectives on the world that **precede observation** and give the believer a sense of coherence about life. However, many religious **believers reject** this view, seeing their assertions as cognitive in nature. They believe that they (and the founders of their religions) have observed God/the Divine at work in the world and therefore they possess much more than a 'perspective' or 'attitude'.

☐ **Controversy 3:** *Religious assertions are* **verifiable – in the end!**
Is it really true that there is no way to verify a religious assertion? Or, to use Flew's approach, that religious assertions always become qualified to the point of meaninglessness? Many religious believers appeal to **traditional arguments** for the existence of God which make use of observations of the empirical world. Basil Mitchell uses the parable of the stranger to show that there is evidence for both belief and non-belief, which is why religious believers exercise **faith**. However, Anthony Flew would see this as a set of **qualifications** that does indeed make religious assertions meaningless.

Sp●tlight: **Evaluative judgements**

This section contains a special insight that you can use to form a judgement.

It is difficult to think that Moses, Jesus, Muhammad or the Buddha would accept that the truths they proclaimed were based on their respective 'bliks', which led them to insights and observations. It is easier to believe that these figures believed themselves to have had direct (observable, real) encounters with Ultimate Reality which led them to view the world in a different way.

Issue:

How far logical positivism should be accepted as providing a valid criterion for meaning in the use of language

- **Controversy 1: *All knowledge* cannot be reduced *to scientific and logical formulations!***

  The objective of the logical positivists was to establish, as Tillich observed, a '**clearing house**' through which all statements could be sorted into: (i) analytic propositions (a priori statements, true by definition), (ii) synthetic statements (a posteriori propositions, established by observation and (iii) meaningless statements of 'non-sense'. Without such a clearing house, scientific and rational progress would be held back. However, it can be argued that this 'clearing house' is **too small** to contain the scope of human development. For, fiction, poetry, art and imagination have long taught and inspired humanity, shaping **values**, attitudes and actions.

- **Controversy 2: *Modifications* to logical positivism show *its inadequacy!***

  Ayer noted that a strict insistence on directly observable experience to establish synthetic propositions was deficient. For, this would render problematic any claim about a past event) or any scientific law. In the first case, we do not have the ability, and in the second case, we do not have the time to observe every instance. This led to Ayer's introduction of a '**weak form**' of verification – statements can be supported by general observations about sense data. However, this has **opened the door** to faith eventually yielding verification (B. Mitchell) and John Hick's view that a proposition can be 'eschatologically verified'. These developments not only show the original strong form of verification by the logical positivists to have been **deficient** but also point to dangers when modifications are made.

- **Controversy 3: *Logical positivism is* self-defeating!**

  The principle of verification, namely, that all meaningful propositions are either those that are logically necessary (if analytic) or empirically verifiable (if synthetic) is itself an **unverifiable** assertion. This means that it fails as a synthetic statement, since it cannot be proven to be true by observation. Furthermore, if it is a tautology (a statement true by definition), then it is a purely **arbitrary** viewpoint. In either case, it would be foolish to grant authority to logical positivism as a path to determine the meaning of language. However, even though the principle of verification is meaningless, it could be seen as a **recommendation** for the practice of scientific knowledge. It has authority because when it has been employed, science has advanced and superstition has receded.

⁶TRIGGER QUOTES⁹

The traditional disputes of philosophers are, for the most part, as unwarranted as they are unfruitful. **(A. J. Ayer)**

... this clearing house is a very small room, perhaps only a corner of a house, and not a real house. **(P. Tillich)**

Logical positivism is a very attractive view for people who do not want to worry about what they cannot observe. **(T. Maudlin)**

... no matter how many stakes are driven through its [logical positivism's] heart, it arises unbidden in the minds of scientists. **(T. Maudlin)**

Sp⬤tlight: Evaluative judgements

This section contains a special insight that you can use to form a judgement.

Ludwig Wittgenstein warned against a society which only turned to science in order to learn and to the arts for pleasure. He felt that we are impoverished if we ignore the insights of poets, artists, musicians and others who share views on life outside of what can be verified by empirical observation.

TIP

When presenting controversies, always refer to key terms, theorists and sources rather than merely presenting your own opinions.

AO1 Trigger revision activity

A

ZIP

Logical positivism and verification

---

1 There are no Triggers in this zip file! Find and add in the relevant Triggers. ➡

2 Now put the Triggers in the same order as they appear in the AO1 section above. ➡

3 Practise 'downloading' your zip file of Triggers from memory. See how many you can recall on first attempt.

6 Now read through your definitions and think about ways in which you could develop these using your Trigger quotes. ⬅

5 Attempt to write one clear sentence to define each Trigger. ⬅

4 When you are confident enough, order the Triggers into a list as you may do in an examination situation.

B

ZIP

Falsification and challenges

Falsification	
falsification	wisdom's parable
meaningless	count against
theory to observation	evidence
religious assertion	tautology
qualify	changed the assertion
non-falsifiable	

Criticisms of Verification and Falsification	
not itself verifiable	precede observation
not an empirical	faith
arbitrary	parable of the stranger
deficiency	Swinburne
eschatological verification	toys
overall perspective	cannot use observation
blik	

---

1 Here is your zip file of portable Triggers. ➡

2 Practise 'downloading' your zip file of Triggers from memory. See how many you can recall on first attempt. ➡

3 When you are confident enough, order the Triggers into a list as you may do in an examination situation.

5 Now read through your descriptions and think about ways in which you could develop these using your Trigger quotes. ⬅

4 Attempt to write one clear sentence to define each Trigger. ⬅

AO2 Trigger revision activity

 A ZIP

Persuasiveness of arguments on meaning/ meaninglessness of religious language

| verifiable – in the beginning, traditional arguments, faith, qualification | non-cognitive, overall perspective, precede observation, monism | winged angels, verify, observation, hate |

1 Find the unhelpful Triggers! **This zip file contains several inappropriate or irrelevant Triggers**. Find these and replace them with the real Triggers from the AO2 section.

2 There's another problem: the Triggers are out of order! Put them in the same order as they appear in the AO2 section above.

3 Practise 'downloading' your zip file of Triggers from memory. See how many you can recall on first attempt.

6 Now read through all your sentences and think about ways in which you could develop these using your Trigger quotes, further examples, and noting strengths and weaknesses.

5 Attempt to write one clear sentence to define each Trigger.

4 When you are confident enough, order the Triggers into a list as you may do in an examination situation.

 B ZIP

Logical positivism as valid

| cannot be reduced, clearing house, too small, values | modifications, weak form, opened the door, deficient | self defeating! unverifiable, arbitrary, recommendation |

1 Here is your zip file of portable Triggers.

2 Practise 'downloading' your zip file of Triggers from memory. See how many you can recall on first attempt.

3 When you are confident enough, order the Triggers into a list as you may do in an examination situation.

5 Now read through all your sentences and think about ways in which you could develop these using your Trigger quotes, further examples, and noting strengths and weaknesses.

4 'Double-click' each Trigger in your memory – what can you say about an evaluative point of view in a clear sentence? Write this down. Do this for each Trigger in turn.

 **TIP**

Why Trigger?
Remember, your Triggers are to help you transfer your knowledge and understanding in a manageable, efficient and portable manner.

Religious language

AO1

What is ... Knowledge and understanding ?

This is the skill that involves *selecting* the relevant and appropriate information, *organising* it and then *presenting* it through a *personal explanation* that may involve the use of supporting *evidence* and *examples*.

Aquinas believed in a relationship between our experience and a greater reality – but this is not a literal relationship that can be explained through univocal language. For, God is beyond human experience.

6 TRIGGER QUOTES 9

Univocal terms mean absolutely the same thing, but equivocal terms absolutely different. **(T. Aquinas)**

The names said of God and creatures are predicated neither univocally nor equivocally but analogically ... **(T. Aquinas)**

... our intellect ... in order to understand God, forms conceptions proportional to the perfections flowing from God to creatures. **(T. Aquinas)**

Theme 4C: Religious language as non-cognitive and analogical

Aquinas and analogy

- Thomas Aquinas explored the possibility of speaking about God, given that God is, essentially, **unknowable**.
- **Univocal** language has the same meaning in different contexts. For example, 'carpet' can mean the same thing whether we are talking about a living room carpet or a carpet in a mosque.
- **Aquinas rejects** the view that language for God can be used univocally because God cannot be reduced to the language of time and causation.
- This leaves the possibility that the language of God is **equivocal**; equivocal language is language which has wholly different meanings when the context changes. For example, 'set' can refer to a television or a series of repetitions when working on physical fitness.
- Believing that our language about God is equivocal means, for example, that there is **no correspondence** between the meaning of 'good' as we use it to describe any person, place or thing and when we use this same word to describe God.
- Aquinas also rejects this view because we live in **relationship** to God: we know causes, we know God's created world and we have been created by God.
- Aquinas says that the compromise between these two positions is **analogy**. An analogy is a comparison between one thing and another which is based on the idea that there is a partial similarity.
- The analogy of **proportion** states that we share aspects of a common nature to God since we are made in her/his **image**. However, it is only in proportion to God's nature.
- When we say that God is powerful, we mean that God has that nature totally (omnipotence), but we have that nature only in proportion to being human beings (i.e. we are not omnipotent).
- However, we have some understanding from **our experience** of power of what it means to say that God is omnipotent.
- In a similar way, the analogy of **attribution** focuses on the fact that we reflect something of the attributes of God (e.g. wisdom).
- We are 'wise', but **not independently** of God; we have insight on God's wisdom because God has created the attribute of wisdom in our lives.

Ramsay's approach

- Ian Ramsay taught that religious claims begin with the **observable world** but do not end there.
- Central to Ramsay's approach is the idea of '**disclosure**'. This is the moment where the 'something more' quality has become conscious.

- For example, a judge who is conducting a court case suddenly realises that the defendant is her old school friend 'Alli'. Thus, a 'normal' work situation contains a 'disclosure' which has made it personally **meaningful**.
- A believer has a similar sense of **discernment** in the midst of everyday situations about the ultimate source and meaning of life.
- A **model** is a quality or situation with which we are familiar (e.g. 'wisdom', 'causation'), but which can be used for reaching another situation with which we are not so familiar.
- A **qualifier** is word which points to a way or direction in which we may understand the model until a moment of discernment occurs. (i.e. 'infinite', 'first', 'eternal').
- Religious believers describe God using models: wise, **shepherd**, powerful – we understand the meaning of these models from everyday life.
- However, believers do not mean these to be interpreted literally: God is beyond everyday life. 'Qualifiers' must be employed to show how the model is being used **differently**.
- For example, God is described as a 'cause' (model). Then, a qualifier is used ('first') to direct one in their interpretation, to ask what caused each cause until one arrives at a mystery. This **mystery** is a moment of discernment in which one apprehends a mystery – God.
- 'God' is the end of this direction of travel; **God includes** all experience and language.
- Ramsay did not believe that a logical formula could establish God as the 'first' cause or as 'infinitely' wise; belief is a discernment that occurs when contemplating a model and its qualifier.

Agreements and disagreements

- Both Ramsay and Aquinas give believers **permission** to use language and concepts with which they are familiar to express their faith.
- Aquinas and Ramsay use language about God from the observable world but **avoid literalism** (univocal language) through the concept of analogy.
- The analogical approach provides a way for non-believers to **understand** religious teaching as insights into a mystery.
- Aquinas' analogies of proportion and attribution mean that believers need not be silent about a transcendent God but can **express** their beliefs.
- Ramsay's discussion of 'discernment' might **relate** to the 'something more' experience of life that many have had.
- **Hume** noted that an analogy is only as good as the point at which two things are similar.
- If one cannot establish the meaning of the word 'God' in the same way in which we establish the meaning of everyday words ('house', 'car', etc.) then the **analogy fails**.
- Both Aquinas and Ramsay assume the existence of God; their views only have weight for those who share their **assumption**.
- If one has no empirical knowledge of God/the Divine yet assumes that God exists, one will have to use language about God equivocally. Therefore, statements about God would be **meaningless**.
- Ramsay's model-qualifier approach only claims to give insights into a 'mystery' rather than give **verifiable** knowledge of God in any way that would satisfy a non-believer.

Quick Revision

Write down three analogies that have nothing to do with religious language. Now, write down three analogies that religious people might use to describe the Divine/God. Explain why these analogies are not using language in a univocal, equivocal, or literalistic way.

Model	Qualifier
Shepherd	All-loving
Cause	First
Wise	Infinitely
Creation	Ex-nihilo

Specification Link

Challenges including how far analogies can give meaningful insights into religious language. A consideration of how these two views (Aquinas/Ramsey) can be used to help understand religious teachings.

Ramsay: truths about God become real in a moment of 'discernment', when we perceive that there is something more going on than our normal observations.

❛TRIGGER QUOTES❜

Neither a catholic nor a pagan knows the very nature of God as it is in itself ...
(T. Aquinas)

We should expect religious language ... to be constructed from object language which has been given appropriately strange qualifications. **(I. Ramsay)**

AO2

What is ... Evaluation and critical analysis ?

The AO2 skills of evaluation and critical analysis mean engaging with the controversies surrounding a subject. This is more than merely describing or listing the points made about a controversy. To achieve this, one weighs up strengths and weaknesses of various sides and takes a position. On the right are three controversies for each issue – you can engage in these by extending their arguments (adding examples, quotes or other details), weighing up their strengths and weaknesses, and coming to a conclusion.

Religious believers view logical positivism as too 'reductive', condemning too many sources of human knowledge as 'nonsense'. Defenders of logical positivism say that we need to 'boil away' superstitions which have held humanity back.

❛TRIGGER QUOTES❜

'God' is a key word, an irreducible posit, an ultimate of explanation of the kind of commitment he professes. **(I. Ramsay)**

[the believer] is obliged to use, for the expression of his beliefs, language governed by paradoxical rules. **(I. Crombie)**

There are, indeed, things that cannot be put into words. They make themselves manifest. They are what is mystical.
(L. Wittgenstein)

Issue:

To what extent do the challenges to logical positivism provide convincing arguments to non-religious believers?

Three evaluative controversies!

- ☐ **Controversy 1:** *Logical positivism can never be convincing?*
  Logical positivism clearly defines which statements can be meaningful: those that are **analytic or synthetic**. Any challenge that comes from a statement outside of this scope would have to be seen as either illogical or, literally, '**non-sense**'. This position has been built on Hume's empiricism and has won wide support because it can be seen as the foundation of scientific progress. However, this approach rules out the possibility of knowledge from the fields of music, ethics and aesthetics – not to mention religion. Thus, logical positivism is too **reductive**.

- ☐ **Controversy 2:** *Analogical approaches make more sense than logical positivism?*
  One can appreciate logical positivism especially in relation to **simplistic, literalistic** religious statements such as, 'God created the world in seven 24-hour days'. However, an analogical approach is appealing because it gives religious statements a cognitive status as an observation on the world without having to take these statements as literally true. This means that religious language is a point of contact with a larger **mystery**. However, if there is no way to verify the supposed similarity between any metaphysical claim in relation to the observable world, then the analogical approach **yields no meaning**.

- ☐ **Controversy 3:** *Wittgenstein's journey challenges logical positivism?*
  Early in his career, Wittgenstein met with the Vienna Circle and advanced views which aligned with their convictions. For instance, Wittgenstein only considered language to be meaningful insofar as it provided an **accurate picture** of reality as known by the senses. However, he came to the view that language should be viewed as a meaningful activity according to the roles it plays in the lives of its speakers. Thus, we need to know what it means to those using it (**meaning is found in use**). However, the danger of this view is that it can lead to a **'relativistic swamp'** in which any statement could be said to be 'true'.

Sp🔵tlight: Evaluative judgements

This section contains a special insight that you can use to form a judgement.

A recent way to try to prove the meaningfulness of religious views as cognitive claims has been to use the 'proof' of near-death experiences (NDEs). Those reporting NDEs claim to have out of body experiences with similar features (floating, going down a tunnel, seeing a bright light, etc.). This is said to affirm religious doctrines on life after death as analogical language. However, there are naturalistic explanations for these experiences (i.e. when blood stops circulating to the brain, one experiences a 'floating' sensation).

Issue:

Whether non-cognitive interpretations are valid responses to the challenges to the meaning of religious language

- **Controversy 1: *Communication that's non-cognitive works!***
  The point of language is to support communication between human beings so that they can work together with **shared meaning**. One way to achieve this is through cognitive language based on verifiable or falsifiable experiences. Yet, the fact that so many religious believers can **communicate meaningfully** with one another using analogy and non-verifiable concepts such as 'soul', 'God', 'paradise', etc., shows that non-cognitive communication works. Of course, this **ignores** a significant segment of the population for which this language is meaningless and who require cognitive statements that can be verified.

- **Controversy 2: *Viewing religious language as non-cognitive doesn't work* for religious believers!**
  In his reaction to Hare's 'blik' approach, Anthony Flew noted that **religious believers** view their assertions as cognitive. Furthermore, John Hick has noted that the **founders** of the world religions would have never accepted that their insights on the Divine were non-cognitive. However, it could be argued that religious believers are **confused** in that they think they are speaking cognitively, when in fact they are using non-cognitive language (or, 'memes') that they have gained through their family, communities and culture. This language is a creation of the contexts in which they have been raised and does not correspond to verifiable experience.

- **Controversy 3: *A compromise can be reached!***
  Hare's approach has identified that we often have an **overall perspective** or attitude toward life which determines how we view the '**data**'. One way to interpret his insight is to say that religious believers make cognitive statements and conclusions from a non-cognitive standpoint. In other words, their insights and observations use cognitive language but emerge from a non-cognitive perspective or blik. However, if this is true, then one could **test** or verify the observations and come to a conclusion of the truth-value of the supposed non-cognitive perspective – meaning that it was never a non-cognitive perspective in the first place.

TIP

If you decide to use a Trigger quote in an exam response, always take time to briefly explain what the quote means and how it fits into your argument.

Quick Revision

Create a debate in a dialogue form between a religious believer who accepts that their beliefs express an attitude for which there is no final proof and a religious believer who believes that their beliefs are founded on objective reality. Have your characters refer to scholars from this theme. This will help you with an exam evaluation question in this area.

Spotlight: Evaluative judgements

This section contains a special insight that you can use to form a judgement.

Flew said that statements should be viewed as meaningless if there is nothing that could count against them. However, people find meaning in many statements which cannot be proved or disproved in sense experience. One example of this are the many interfaith dialogue events that occur between religions. The fact that agreement is sometimes reached on metaphysical beliefs which cross religion, culture and creed shows the power of religious statements to communicate meaning. Of course, the fact that agreement is not often reached could be seen to support Flew's point of view!

⦿ TRIGGER QUOTES ⦿

Our whole commerce with the world depends on our blik about the world ...
(R. Hare)

I am against religion because it teaches us to be satisfied with not understanding the world.   **(R. Dawkins)**

If Hare's religion really is a blik, involving no cosmological assertions ... then surely he is not a Christian at all?   **(A. Flew)**

AO1 Trigger revision activity

A · ZIP

Aquinas and analogy

unknowable, univocal, Aquinas rejects, equivocal, no correspondence, relationship

analogy, proportion, image, our experience, attribution, not independently

1 Here is your zip file of portable Triggers.

2 Practise 'downloading' your zip file of Triggers from memory. See how many you can recall on first attempt.

3 When you are confident enough, order the Triggers into a list as you may do in an examination situation.

5 Now read through your descriptions and think about ways in which you could develop these using your Trigger quotes.

4 Attempt to write one clear sentence to define each Trigger.

TIP

Why Trigger?
Remember, your Triggers are to help you transfer your knowledge and understanding in a manageable, efficient and portable manner.

B · ZIP

Ramsay and Agreements and disagreements

Ramsay	Agreements and disagreements
shepherd, disclosure, differently, qualifier, observable world, mystery, meaningful, God includes	verifiable, understand, Hume, relate, express, analogy fails, avoid literalism, permission

1 Fix the zip file! There are four Triggers missing from this zip file – find them and add them in.

2 There's another problem: the Triggers are out of order! Put them in the same order as they appear in the AO1 section above.

3 Practise 'downloading' your zip file of Triggers from memory. See how many you can recall on first attempt.

6 Now read through your definitions and think about ways in which you could develop these using your Trigger quotes.

5 Attempt to write one clear sentence to define each Trigger.

4 When you are confident enough, order the Triggers into a list as you may do in an examination situation.

AO2 Trigger revision activity

 A

ZIP

Are challenges to logical positivism convincing?

| can never be convincing, analytic or synthetic, non-sense, reductive | analogical approaches, simplistic literalistic, mystery, yields no meaning | Wittgenstein's journey, accurate picture, meaning is found in use, relativistic swamp |

1 Here is your zip file of portable Triggers.

2 Practise 'downloading' your zip file of Triggers from memory. See how many you can recall on first attempt.

3 When you are confident enough, order the Triggers into a list as you may do in an examination situation.

5 Now read through all your sentences and think about ways in which you could develop these using your Trigger quotes, further examples, and noting strengths and weaknesses.

4 'Double-click' each Trigger in your memory – what can you say about an evaluative point of view in a clear sentence? Write this down. Do this for each Trigger in turn.

 TIP

When you use a Trigger Quote in an exam response, make sure that you include an explanation on how it is relevant to the question.

 B

ZIP

The validity of non-cognitive approaches to religious language

| non-cognitive doesn't work, founders, confused | compromise, overall perspective, data | non-cognitive works, communicate meaningfully, ignores |

1 Fix the zip file! There are three Triggers missing from this zip file – find them and add them in.

2 There's another problem: the Triggers are out of order! Put them in the same order as they appear in the AO2 section above.

3 Practise 'downloading' your zip file of Triggers from memory. See how many you can recall on first attempt.

6 Now read through all your sentences and think about ways in which you could develop these using your Trigger quotes, further examples, and noting strengths and weaknesses.

5 Attempt to write one clear sentence to define each Trigger.

4 When you are confident enough, order the Triggers into a list as you may do in an examination situation.

Specification Link

Functions of symbols (John Randall).

AO1

What is ... Knowledge and understanding ?

This is the skill that involves *selecting* the relevant and appropriate information, *organising* it and then *presenting* it through a *personal explanation* that may involve the use of supporting *evidence* and *examples*.

Randall compared the study of religion to the study of art – each discipline can enhance our understanding of humanity.

❝TRIGGER QUOTES❞

All ideas of God, indeed like all religious beliefs, are religious symbols. **(J. Randall)**

Symbols do not tell us anything that is verifiably so, they rather make us see something about our experience ...

(J. Randall)

Specification Link

God as that which concerns us ultimately (Paul Tillich).

Theme 4D: **Religious language as non-cognitive and symbolic**

Randall's approach

- John Randall was a **philosopher** who viewed religion as a human phenomenon.
- Religious language **communicates knowledge**, but not the type of factual (cognitive) knowledge that the empirical sciences convey.
- Religion deals with the **non-cognitive** dimension of human experience. It does this through the use of symbols.
- Randall accepted Tillich's understanding of a **symbol** as something which points beyond itself to a deeper reality.
- However, Randall was a **non-realist**, that is, he did not see these symbols as pointing to a reality beyond humanity; they serve the valuable function of expressing human views, emotions and actions.
- Religion provides **insight** on what it means to exist as a being in the universe.
- Like science or art, religion makes a **valuable contribution** to society, though it has more similarities with art than science as it opens up meanings that can be explored.
- As a distinct field of study, religion has a **body of knowledge** different than other disciplines – this is its symbols and myths which emerge from its historical records along with current beliefs and practices.
- We can understand religion by understanding how symbols **function**:

Four functions of religious symbols	
They **arouse** emotion and stir to action	Symbols strengthen people's commitment to what they feel is right.
They **bind** a community together	A group of people may view a symbol together and thereby deepen their bond to one another.
They **communicate** qualities of experience	Just as art opens up pathways of communication not available through mathematics, so also do religious symbols.
They foster and **clarify** our human experience	Religious symbols provide a pathway for people to express an 'order of splendour' they experience.

Tillich's approach

- Paul Tillich was a **theologian**, known as an 'apostle to the sceptics' for defining God and faith in existential terms.
- Tillich defined God as that which concerns us ultimately, and faith as the state of '**ultimate concern**'. However, God is not a 'being' like other beings; God is the **ground of being itself**.

- Other terms that Tillich used for God were '**unconditional**', 'infinite' and 'ultimate'.
- Reality has many levels; the language that is adequate for the mathematical sciences is not the most adequate for **grasping** the level of 'being-itself'.
- Only religious language can express matters of ultimate concern; it needs to use **symbols** since that which is transcendent is always beyond our direct understanding.
- A symbol points to a reality beyond itself and **participates** in that reality.
- For example, consider a nation's **flag**. The many rules about how flags are to be treated reveal that it is more than a piece of cloth – it participates in a reality beyond itself.
- A symbol also **opens up** levels of reality and evokes a response. Consider a landscape painting by Reubens with its balance, colour, weighting. It opens up reality that could not be experienced in any other way.
- Symbols are born from **collective unconsciousness** and can die. A group must say an unconscious 'yes' before something can become a symbol.
- Religious symbols are symbols of the ultimate ground of being; the transcendent always **lies beyond** symbols.
- When symbols become mistaken for the reality in which they participate, they become idols. **Idolatry** is the absolutising of the symbol.
- God is both a symbol and not a symbol. **God is always beyond** the symbol, but we need symbols (attributes and actions of God) in order to relate to the transcendent.
- We cannot have a relationship with something that is **utterly transcendent**. So, as soon as we form any idea of a perfect being, we are dealing with the world of symbols.

Challenges and understandings

- Randall views religious language as the **creation of humans**; therefore, it can only give insights about humans, not God or any transcendent reality.
- As non-cognitive language, symbolic language fails the tests of both **verification** and falsification and therefore has to be viewed as both 'non-sense' and meaningless by those who take an empirical approach to knowledge.
- Tillich's views have been labelled a '**philosophical confusion**' (Paul Edwards) because Tillich acknowledged that God cannot be spoken of in literal terms, but then went on to say quite a bit about God.
- As **symbols change** their meaning over time, how can they provide correct spiritual insight? Are they not hostage to history?
- Many religious believers view religious teachings as depicting reality as it '**really is**'; they would therefore reject Randall's non-realism and Tillich's view that language about God is symbolic in nature.
- Randall provides an important corrective to a hasty dismissal of ancient theology: many **reflective ancients** did not view the meaning of their rituals and religious objects in literal terms.
- Randall provides a way to study the phenomenon of religion – through symbols and their history. Like the discipline of **art history**, a study of religious symbols can deepen our understanding of humanity.
- Tillich gives the believer a way of speaking about God without thinking that their statements can '**capture**' God.
- Tillich understands the religious tendency to **idolatry** – forgetting that there is a reality beyond the symbol.

❛**TRIGGER** QUOTES❜

Everything in time and space has become at some time a symbol of the Holy. (**P. Tillich**)

Faith is the state of being ultimately concerned. (**P. Tillich**)

Religiously speaking, god transcends his own name. (**P. Tillich**)

The statement that God is being-itself is a nonsymbolic statement. It does not point beyond itself. (**P. Tillich**)

TIP

If you are overwhelmed by the number of Triggers, then create a smaller list which will 'trigger' just as much knowledge.

Specification Link

Challenges including whether a symbol is adequate or gives the right insights. A consideration of how these two views (Randall/Tillich) can be used to help understand religious teachings.

❛**TRIGGER** QUOTES❜

Religion gives valuable insights into what it means to exist as a being in the universe. (**J. Randall**)

... it is like art, which likewise furnishes no supplementary truth, but it does open whole worlds to be explored. (**J. Randall**)

Whatever we say about that which concerns us ultimately, whether or not we call it God, has a symbolic meaning. (**P. Tillich**)

When a sentence contains an irreducible metaphor, it follows at once that the sentence is devoid of cognitive meaning ... (**P. Edwards**)

AO2

What is ... Evaluation and critical analysis ?

The AO2 skills of evaluation and critical analysis mean engaging with the controversies surrounding a subject. This is more than merely describing or listing the points made about a controversy. To achieve this, one weighs up strengths and weaknesses of various sides and takes a position. On the right are three controversies for each issue – you can engage in these by extending their arguments (adding examples, quotes or other details), weighing up their strengths and weaknesses, and coming to a conclusion.

TRIGGER QUOTES

The language of faith is the language of symbols. **(P. Tillich)**

A religion is a system of symbols which acts to establish powerful, pervasive, and long-lasting moods ... **(C Geertz)**

Quick Revision

Write down all the reasons you can think of as to why using symbols is necessary and then, all the reasons why using symbols is not necessary. Which list is more impressive to you? Write out your answer to this question with a justification. This will help you with an exam evaluation question in this area.

Issue:

Whether symbolic language can be agreed as having adequate meaning as a form of language

Three evaluative controversies!

- **Controversy 1: *Symbolic language opens up deeper layers of life?***
  Paul Tillich viewed the language of **mathematics as inadequate** to make sense of much that we encounter in life. Symbols express our ultimate concerns, providing insight, guidance and **inspiration** – such as what can be found when we gaze at a beautiful painting. Yet, 'layers of life' is a vague phrase which cannot be analysed in any objective way. We are far better off, and we will make more progress in our lives, by remaining in the only 'layer' which can be verified: the **empirical world** of the senses.

- **Controversy 2: *Entire societies find symbolic language meaningful.***
  Symbolic language works to express **common understanding** (Tillich's insights about a nation's flag). Not only this, symbolic language motivates groups by **creating cohesion** and the will to act (Randall's four functions). Yet, Tillich admits that symbols grow and die – they are **not constant nor consistent** in their meanings. This means that we can never be certain that a symbol means the same thing as it did to a past generation – or even to the person next to us.

- **Controversy 3: *Tillich vs. Randall: no adequate agreement.***
  There is a huge difference between these two scholars who promote the value of symbolic language: Randall is a **non-realist** (symbolic language is entirely a human creation), whereas Tillich believes that through symbolic language we can participate in a **transcendent world**. This difference shows the weakness of this approach to meaning. Furthermore, many religious people would reject the views of both scholars, believing that religious teaching is not symbolic in nature, but has **objective, cognitive** meaning.

Spotlight: Evaluative judgements

This section contains a special insight that you can use to form a judgement.

When one says that they have been inspired by or learned valuable lessons from a fantasy film, a novel, painting or a piece of poetry, they are bearing witness to the power of symbols to convey meaning. Yet, any attempt to convey how this meaning can inspire others can be easily rejected as subjective and non-verifiable, thus pointing to the inadequacy of this language to convey meaning.

Issue:

How far the works of Randall and Tillich provide a suitable counter-challenge to logical positivism

- **Controversy 1:** *The logical positivist language room is too small!*
  Randall and Tillich seek to enlarge the amount of language that can be counted as meaningful through examining human attitudes, feelings and emotions as expressed through symbols. This is an attractive approach because all human beings express themselves in these areas and consider their assertions to hold **meaning**. Yet, logical positivists would argue that aeons of exploring symbolic meaning has kept humanity trapped in **superstition**. Progress should be measured by the amount of language we devote to **analytic or synthetic** statements; all other language should be accorded a lower status.

- **Controversy 2:** *Symbols are of ambiguous value for humans!*
  It is difficult to deny Randall's point that symbols unite human communities and stir people to action. One need look no further than at a **flag** held up a the front of a charging army! Yet all of Tillich's lofty language about symbols opening up layers of meaning must be counterbalanced by the fact that symbols have been used to unleash hatred, violence and horror – one need look no further than the **swastika**. This is why a logical positivist may say that we should forsake the exploration of the meaning of symbols for the exploration of the world of the **senses**.

- **Controversy 3:** *Symbols are necessary to express ourselves fully.*
  Not only is symbolic language found everywhere, it allows us, says Randall, to express a dimension of human experience. Randall calls this an **'order of splendour'**, the ability to have a vision of perfection and the possibilities of human life. By rejecting this 'order of splendour' as meaningful, logical positivism denies what most deeply **drives human experience**. Yet, logical positivism only rejects language that does not make logical sense or cannot be verifiable. If a symbol can make sense within an analytic statement or can be verified to have meaning in a synthetic statement then this language would be considered **cognitive language**. If not, it would be deemed meaningless.

 TIP

If you decide to use a Trigger quote in an exam response, always take time to briefly explain what the quote means and how it fits into your argument.

Quick Revision

Write down the names of three different symbols in the religion you are studying. In your own words, describe how each of these symbols: (i) can teach someone outside of that religion something about that religion, (ii) could become an idol for those in that religion and (iii) how that symbol points beyond itself. This will help you with an exam question in this area.

❝TRIGGER QUOTES❞

Symbolic language alone is able to express the ultimate because it transcends the capacity of any finite reality to express it directly. **(P. Tillich)**

Tillich's work failed to satisfy the logical positivist's longing for the empirically verifiable. **(G. Hummel)**

Sp●tlight: Evaluative judgements

This section contains a special insight that you can use to form a judgement.

The study of religion from a sociological point of view (e.g. the number/types of people engaging in a certain ritual) or a psychological point of view (e.g. observing the brain during a religious experience) is compatible with verification as empirical data is central. However, both Randall and Tillich go beyond empirical data. Randall speaks about a level of human experience that is impossible to know apart from our response to symbols and Tillich speaks about 'being itself'.

Tillich said that a nation's flag is a symbol; it participates in a reality greater than itself. Perhaps this explains why there are so many guidelines as to how this object should be treated.

AO1 Trigger revision activity

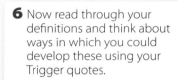

A ZIP

John Randall

valuable contribution	insight	bind
communicates knowledge	arouse	communicate
symbol	function	body of knowledge
non-realist	philosopher	

1 Fix the zip file! There are two Triggers missing from this zip file – find them and add them in.

2 There's another problem: the Triggers are out of order! Put them in the same order as they appear in the AO1 section above.

3 Practise 'downloading' your zip file of Triggers from memory. See how many you can recall on first attempt.

4 When you are confident enough, order the Triggers into a list as you may do in an examination situation.

5 Attempt to write one clear sentence to define each Trigger.

6 Now read through your definitions and think about ways in which you could develop these using your Trigger quotes.

B ZIP

Tillich and Challenges and understandings

1 There are no Triggers in this zip file! Find and add in the relevant Triggers.

2 Now put the Triggers in the same order as they appear in the AO1 section above.

3 Practise 'downloading' your zip file of Triggers from memory. See how many you can recall on first attempt.

4 When you are confident enough, order the Triggers into a list as you may do in an examination situation.

5 Attempt to write one clear sentence to define each Trigger.

6 Now read through your definitions and think about ways in which you could develop these using your Trigger quotes.

AO2 Trigger revision activity

A ZIP

Symbolic language as having adequate meaning

| Entire societies, common understanding, creating cohesion | Tillich vs. Randall, transcendent world, objective, cognitive | Opens up, mathematics as inadequate, empirical world |

1 Fix the zip file! There are three Triggers missing from this zip file – find them and add them in.

2 There's another problem: the Triggers are out of order! Put them in the same order as they appear in the AO2 section above.

3 Practise 'downloading' your zip file of Triggers from memory. See how many you can recall on first attempt.

6 Now read through all your sentences and think about ways in which you could develop these using your Trigger quotes, further examples, and noting strengths and weaknesses.

5 Attempt to write one clear sentence to define each Trigger.

4 When you are confident enough, order the Triggers into a list as you may do in an examination situation.

B ZIP

Randall and Tillich vs. logical positivism

1 There are no Triggers in this zip file! Find and add in the relevant Triggers.

2 Now put the Triggers in the same order as they appear in the AO2 section above.

3 Practise 'downloading' your zip file of Triggers from memory. See how many you can recall on first attempt.

6 Now read through all your sentences and think about ways in which you could develop these using your Trigger quotes, further examples, and noting strengths and weaknesses.

5 Attempt to write one clear sentence to define each Trigger.

4 When you are confident enough, order the Triggers into a list as you may do in an examination situation.

Specification Link

Complex form of mythical language that communicates values and insights into purpose of existence. Supportive evidence – different forms of myths to convey meaning: creation myths. Myths help to overcome fears of the unknown; myths effective way of transmitting religious, social and ethical values.

AO1

What is ...
Knowledge and
understanding

This is the skill that involves *selecting* the relevant and appropriate information, *organising* it and then *presenting* it through a *personal explanation* that may involve the use of supporting *evidence* and *examples*.

Spot the Triggers!
The words in blue are Triggers – key words and phrases that can help you remember knowledge and understanding in this area.

TIP

For some scholars of religion, a fairy tale is merely a popularised or 'degraded' form of a myth. The latter uses supernatural characters to convey transforming truths.

Theme 4E: Religious language as non-cognitive and mythical

Myth: meaning and creation myths

- In the study of religion, a myth is not a **fairy tale** or merely a story with fictional elements. Rather, a myth is an account which **contains truth** conveyed through imagery and symbolism.
- A myth requires one to look beyond a literal interpretation to the meaning of the **symbols**, analogies and metaphors.
- Myths exist in **every culture** and involve stories of creation, gods and goddesses, heroes, and good vs. evil.
- Some believe that **deconstructing** a myth (i.e. attempting to find the 'real', historical account which gave rise to the myth through empirical means) robs a myth of the truth it contains.
- Mythology is nothing less than a form of **literature** that requires understanding and interpretation.
- Understanding the original context or *Sitz im Leben* (German for, 'situation in life') in which the myth was created can help unlock its meaning.
- In the work of **Carl Jung** and others, myths are seen as ways to explore what it means to be human.
- Whilst some religious believers interpret the stories of their religions **literally**, others view them as myths which can instruct us about the divine.
- **Creation myths** are found across religions; the Judeo-Christian creation account shares mythical language with other accounts from the ancient Near East.
- **Water** signified chaos for ancients, as oceans were uncontrollable, unpredictable and uncrossable.
- The mythical theme of bringing order from **chaos** is shown in the Judeo-Christian myth by God calming the waters, dividing them and populating the world with life.
- Bringing order from chaos is symbolised by the bringing of **light from darkness**; light symbolises knowledge, understanding and righteous power and chaos symbolises darkness. All of these themes helped the ancients cope with fears about the unknown.

Bringing order (land/life) from chaos (darkness/water)		
Place	**Character**	**Action**
Egypt	Khepri	Lifts himself from water to bring creation
America – Zuni tribe	Sun father	Brings creation from the waters
Finland	Virgin daughter of the air	Descends to become the water mother
New Zealand	The demigod Maui	Pulled up islands from the ocean's depths

- The **primacy of human beings** within creation is another mythological theme. In the Judeo-Christian myth, humans are the 'crown' of creation, created in the image of God, and given dominion and stewardship.

- As a myth, this account can be seen as providing insight into **human identity** and purpose.

The solar hero

- The **solar hero** saves the world though bringing the life-giving properties of the sun. Moojen Momen identifies **seven elements** of this myth.
- The myth of the solar hero may be described as an '**archetypal**' myth; this is a primitive concept that has been passed through human history. Carl Jung believed archetypal themes are present in the collective unconscious.
- Some scholars believe that the myth of the solar hero is reflected in religious stories of Rama, Siddhartha and Jesus' **resurrection**.
- Others see aspects of the myth in the **cinema**, comics and video games (Star Wars; The Lord of the Rings; Avengers Infinity Wars). These myths teach that, no matter how evil the world has become, good will always **triumph** over evil.

Elements of the solar-hero myth

1. There is a golden age; all is well.
2. The affairs the solar hero and the hero's family (and/or nation) begin to decline.
3. The hero becomes separated from his people.
4. In some versions, the hero descends to an underworld and a struggle against the forces of darkness ensues.
5. The hero wins a great victory, acquiring the means to save humanity.
6. Just as everything is at its darkest, the earth barren, the hero returns and saves the world.
7. There is a new golden age of justice and hope; the sun returns to revive the fertility of the earth.

Challenges to mythical language

- Myths are shared in a wide variety of forms and passed down through the eras because many find them **meaningful**.
- However, mythology is a form of non-cognitive language. Logical positivists insist that meaning is based either on the logical correspondence between concepts (analytic statements) or synthetic assertions for which evidence is required. Mythology is destined to be **meaningless** by this standard.
- The interpretation of myth is entirely **subjective**. We cannot be certain that the meaning given to a myth is the same meaning given to it by the ancients. This lack of clarity infers unreliability.
- Shared themes across myths challenge the **exclusive** notion of truth in religions. For instance, does the fact that the Judeo-Christian God is not the only 'god' to have created order from chaos dilute the claims of Judaism and Christianity?
- Religions would argue that their accounts of creation or heroes are the original and/or true accounts, whereas similar myths are **derivations**.
- **Rudolph Bultmann** believed that modern people cannot accept the literal interpretation of myths. This is because we accept a world of cause and effect in which God cannot be proven to act in space and time.
- However, Bultmann believed we should hold onto the themes of hope, love and self-understanding conveyed though the myth – these bear **witness** to our human journey, thought the myths themselves have no basis in history.

Specification **Link**

Myths of good against evil; heroic myths.

'TRIGGER QUOTES'

No records of the beginning of time exist except in mythology. **(R. Hoffman)**

... myths preserve and transmit the paradigms / the exemplary models, for all the responsible activities in which men engage. **(M. Eliade)**

Myth knows no Now. Events stand still, as it were, from eternity to eternity, though earlier and later differ. **(C. Elsas)**

A long time ago, in a galaxy far, far away ... **(George Lucas, opening words of the Star Wars myth)**

Specification **Link**

Challenges: problem of competing myths; meanings of myths change over time as they reflect the values of society as societal constructs; demythologisation of myths results in varying interpretations, myths often incompatible with scientific understanding of the world.

Quick Revision

Identify one story from the religion you are studying. This may be an account of creation or a hero (e.g. a founder). Write an outline of the main elements of the story. Now, make a list of key words and concepts from this story that could be found in other stories outside of this religion. This will help you with an exam question on mythical language.

AO2

What is ... Evaluation and critical analysis ?

The AO2 skills of evaluation and critical analysis mean engaging with the controversies surrounding a subject. This is more than merely describing or listing the points made about a controversy. To achieve this, one weighs up strengths and weaknesses of various sides and takes a position. On the right are three controversies for each issue – you can engage in these by extending their arguments (adding examples, quotes or other details), weighing up their strengths and weaknesses, and coming to a conclusion.

❛TRIGGER QUOTES❜

Myths ... developed in illiterate cultures, in which stories are the primary form of communication and instruction.   **(C. Elsas)**

Myth relates a sacred history; it relates a history which took place in primordial times.   **(M. Eliade)**

The enlightenment placed myth in the sphere of the irrational ... it represented an infantile stage of humanity ...   **(P. Beaude)**

Mythology is not a lie, mythology is poetry, it is metaphorical.   **(J. Campbell)**

God is a false person whose story runs from the purely mythological to pseudo-philosophical attempts to restate and revise the primitive data.   **(R. Hoffman)**

Religious language is one aspect of the philosophy of language, a vibrant field which explores the relationships between people, their words and the world.

Issue:

The effectiveness of the terms non-cognitive, analogical and mythical as solutions to the problems of religious language

Three evaluative controversies!

◻ **Controversy 1:** *Granting only cognitive language the status of 'meaningful' is a very narrow view of language.*
Our lives are permeated with non-cognitive statements (e.g. 'I love you.') which can neither be verified nor falsified yet are incredibly important to us, **expressing attitudes**, opinions, feelings and/or emotions. One should therefore accept religious language as a meaningful conduit of human expression. However, the label of 'non-cognitive' for religious language only solves one problem to create another: many **religious believers** view the expression of beliefs as **factual, cognitive** statements about the nature of the universe rather than as non-cognitive assertions.

◻ **Controversy 2:** *Analogies are effective at communicating complex ideas in an understandable way.*
We use analogies in **every sphere of life**, including science, to convey truth (i.e. 'our short-term memory is like RAM in a computer'). **Aquinas** believed that though God is beyond full comprehension, the fact that we are related to God means that analogies can be used to understand God. For example, we can think of **God's goodness** as related to our goodness, though on a higher plane. However, **Hume** said that an analogy is only as good as the extent to which the things compared are similar. As the object of religious language (the Divine, nirvana, god, etc.) is beyond scrutiny, analogy fails to convey meaning.

◻ **Controversy 3:** *Myths lead us to universal truths about existence.*
By examining myths across cultures and religions, we can see **common themes** about the human journey: dealing with chaos, finding order and making a heroic journey towards healing and hope. Thus, mythological language is effective at **conveying identity** and purpose – as well as providing inspiration. However, this view of myth is itself subjective, influenced by **Carl Jung** and popular in the twentieth century. We have no way of knowing if ancient interpreters would have made any such claim about mythological language. Thus, this form of language is too **subjective** to convey meaning.

Sp⬤tlight: Evaluative judgements

This section contains a special insight that you can use to form a judgement.

Myths have been told since the beginning of time. They form one's view of the world, are rich in symbolic language and have been passed down from generation to generation. With the rise of science, one way to view mythology is that it represents a childhood or adolescent stage in the development of humanity. In 'adulthood' we need to base our meaning on testable or verifiable hypotheses. However, if this is true, why does myth persist so strongly through popular books and films (Lord of the Rings, Harry Potter, Star Wars, etc.)?

Issue:

The relevance of religious language issues in the 21st century

- **Controversy 1:** *We are not done with metaphysics!*
  The attack of the logical positivists on non-cognitive language as meaningless encompassed not only religious statements, but **moral and aesthetic** ones as well – all are to be considered metaphysical and therefore meaningless. Yet, despite the popularity of **Ayer's views** in the mid twentieth century, discussions of all three areas (morality, aesthetics and religion) is 'alive and well' as is evidenced by the lively **debate surrounding** 'The God Delusion', ethical issues such as abortion and euthanasia and forcefully expressed opinions on art and architecture in the public sphere.

- **Controversy 2:** *The philosophy of language is in its infancy!*
  Rather than ending discussion of what constitutes meaningfulness in language, the attack on metaphysical assertions by verificationists and falsificationists can be seen as the beginning of an intense period in the development of the **philosophy of language**. For example, **deconstructionism** proposes that there is no unmediated expression of anything non-linguistic in any literary work. Many argue against this (i.e. that knowledge of the objective world can be conveyed). Religious language is a continuing part of this discussion with many arguing that its **language is a 'world view'** which does or does not convey objective reality beyond the text.

- **Controversy 3:** *The fact of pluralism intensifies issues of religious language for religious adherents.*
  Immigration, travel opportunities and a diversity of world views available on multiple media platforms has increased an **awareness of religions** and world views. This has contributed to a **study of symbols**, metaphors and myths across the world's religious traditions. This, in turn, gave rise to the popularity of Paul Tillich, Carl Jung, John Hick and others who have explored non-literalistic approaches to religious language. These developments have caused some adherents to turn to exclusivist and literalistic approaches and has opened up others to inclusivistic and metaphorical approaches – in both cases issues of the meaning religious language is more '**on the table**' than it has ever been. However, it could be argued that this pluralism will eventually yield a secularism in which religious language will be viewed as superfluous.

Sp⊙tlight: Evaluative judgements

This section contains a special insight that you can use to form a judgement.

The extent to which religious language is relevant may be determined by one's view of revelation. (i) If one believes that direct, propositional knowledge of a divine realm is revealed in sacred writings, then issues of religious language may not be a concern. (ii) If one believes that revelation involves myth, metaphor, analogy and symbol because there can be no direct knowledge of the divine realm, then issues of religious language are relevant. (iii) If one believes there is no such thing as revelation, then issues of religious language may be seen as irrelevant.

❛TRIGGER QUOTES❜

Myth expresses ... the understanding that man has of himself in relation to the foundation and the limit of his existence. **(P. Ricoeur)**

The cosmology of the New Testament is essentially mythical in character. The world is viewed as a three-storied structure. **(R. Bultmann)**

The difference between a God who has none of the attributes of his myth and a God who does not exist is 0. **(R. Hoffman)**

Quick Revision

Choose one myth either from the religion you are studying or from the cinema. Write one paragraph on how this myth contains truths valuable for people today. Then, write one paragraph on how this myth is nothing but a form of entertainment, distracting one from 'real life'. Use terminology from Ayer, Hume and others. This will help you with an exam evaluation question on the value of viewing religious declarations as non-cognitive language.

TIP

When presenting controversies always refer to key terms, theorists and sources rather than merely presenting your own opinions.

❛TRIGGER QUOTES❜

It is a sure sign that culture has reached a dead end when it is no longer intrigued by its myths. **(G. Marcus)**

Words strain, Crack and sometimes break, under the burden, Under the tension, slip slide perish, Decay with imprecision, will not stay in place ... **(T. S. Eliot)**

AO1 Trigger revision activity

A ZIP

The meaning of myths and Creation myths

1 There are no Triggers in this zip file! Find and add in the relevant Triggers.

2 Now put the Triggers in the same order as they appear in the AO1 section above.

3 Practise 'downloading' your zip file of Triggers from memory. See how many you can recall on first attempt.

6 Now read through your definitions and think about ways in which you could develop these using your Trigger quotes.

5 Attempt to write one clear sentence to define each Trigger.

4 When you are confident enough, order the Triggers into a list as you may do in an examination situation.

B ZIP

Solar hero myths and Challenges to myth

Hero myths		Challenges to myth	
tape cassette	Jesus' resurrection	Rudolph Bultmann	derivations
archetypal	lunar hero	nasty	meaningful
seven elements	triumph	subjective	inclusive
		witness	

1 Find the unhelpful Triggers! **This zip file contains several inappropriate or irrelevant Triggers**. Find these and replace them with the real Triggers from the AO1 section.

2 There's another problem: the Triggers are out of order! Put them in the same order as they appear in the AO1 section above.

3 Practise 'downloading' your zip file of Triggers from memory. See how many you can recall on first attempt.

6 Now read through your definitions and think about ways in which you could develop these using your Trigger quotes.

5 Attempt to write one clear sentence to define each Trigger.

4 When you are confident enough, order the Triggers into a list as you may do in an examination situation.

AO2 Trigger revision activity

A ZIP

The terms 'non-cognitive', 'analogical' and 'mythical' as solutions to the problems of religious language.

1 There are no Triggers in this zip file! Find and add in the relevant Triggers.

2 Now put the Triggers in the same order as they appear in the AO2 section above.

3 Practise 'downloading' your zip file of Triggers from memory. See how many you can recall on first attempt.

6 Now read through all your sentences and think about ways in which you could develop these using your Trigger quotes, further examples, and noting strengths and weaknesses.

5 Attempt to write one clear sentence to define each Trigger.

4 When you are confident enough, order the Triggers into a list as you may do in an examination situation.

B ZIP

Relevance of religious language issues

The fact of pluralism, awareness of retail, study of symbols, 'on the table'

In its infancy, philosophy of language, architecture, language is a world view

Not done with metaphysics, time lord, Ayer's views, debate surrounding

1 Find the unhelpful Triggers! **This zip file contains several inappropriate or irrelevant Triggers**. Find these and replace them with the real Triggers from the AO2 section.

2 There's another problem: the Triggers are out of order! Put them in the same order as they appear in the AO2 section above.

3 Practise 'downloading' your zip file of Triggers from memory. See how many you can recall on first attempt.

6 Now read through all your sentences and think about ways in which you could develop these using your Trigger quotes, further examples, and noting strengths and weaknesses.

5 Attempt to write one clear sentence to define each Trigger.

4 When you are confident enough, order the Triggers into a list as you may do in an examination situation.

Theme 4F: Religious language as a language game

Language games

AO1

What is ... Knowledge and understanding?

This is the skill that involves *selecting* the relevant and appropriate information, *organising* it and then *presenting* it through a *personal explanation* that may involve the use of supporting *evidence* and *examples*.

Spot the Triggers!
The words in blue are Triggers – key words and phrases that can help you remember knowledge and understanding in this area.

TIP

How comprehensible is a football game to someone who does not understand the meaning of the language (verbal and nonverbal) used by those playing – and watching?

- Ludwig Wittgenstein was a philosopher whose thinking underwent dramatic changes. However, one theme remained central: problems of philosophy occur because of a **misunderstanding** of language.
- Wittgenstein's early work reflects the influence of Bertrand Russell and the **logical positivists**: language must correspond to reality as defined by the physical senses.
- Religious and ethical discussion lies outside of the boundaries of sense, so discussion of these areas is not possible. However, unlike the logical positivists, Wittgenstein did not mean this as a criticism. One needs to have a **respectful stance** in the face of what cannot be discussed.
- Wittgenstein later came to the view that the essence of language is not found in its being an accurate picture of the world, but in the **roles** that it plays in the lives of its speakers.
- Language has no single essence; it is a vast collection of different **practices**, each with its own logic.
- If one wants to understand what others are saying, one needs to understand the **rules** and practices that give rise to the language they are using.
- For example, it is very difficult to understand what is happening at a **football game** or on a construction site unless one comprehends a myriad of terms and phrases that have been given meaning by those communities.
- The meaning of words and phrases depends on the '**form of life**' in which the speakers are engaged.
- A form of life is a **community consensus** of linguistic and non-linguistic behaviours.
- In this consensus of meaning, all language has **coherence**. That is, language 'fits together' in a natural and intelligible way for a particular community.
- Wittgenstein expressed this idea through the concept of '**language games**'; these are communicative activities guided by community rules.
- When we understand the rules of the game, then we can understand the statements of others.
- We cannot understand the meaning of language unless we understand the practices and rules that have shaped it.
- The language game concept is important because it asserts that there are rules of language other than '**fact stating**'.
- 'Fact-stating' language governs **scientific enquiry**; it would be a mistake to force all language into this model in order to make it meaningful.

- **Religious practice** is a form of life and the role of language within that form (for example, in worship) is very different from that of 'fact stating' language.
- For instance, D. Z Philips says that when a believer says, '**eternal life**', she/he may not be stating what they believe to be a scientific fact (i.e. 'I have a life that will go on forever, into infinity'). Instead, they may be expressing that they have a 'kind' of life or a certain '**quality of life**'. One would not know which was the case if one did not understand the rules of the game.
- Games share a '**family resemblance**' that is, rather than there being one common feature between all games, they are connected by overlapping similarities.
- Different forms of life have a 'family resemblance'. One should not think that there is one feature that unlocks the meaning between different forms of life. One has to '**play the game**' in order to learn the meaning attached to words.
- One of the major implications of Wittgenstein's work is that, in contrast to Descartes and much of the Western philosophical tradition, private subjective experience is not the starting point of knowledge. **Knowledge is formed publicly**, in community experience.

Challenges to the language games approach

- **Is the language game concept a form of** anti-realism? One criticism that can be made of Wittgenstein is that his views commit him to **relativism**: if every community has a 'truth' and one cannot know that truth without playing the community's game, then we have no way to say that a statement is true or false. If this is true, then (i) meaningful conversations between different communities cannot occur – **dialogue is impossible**. (ii) Any claim by a religion that a belief is empirically verifiable must be misguided, not understanding the relativistic nature of truth-claims. Many believers would resent the implication that their faith was 'blind', not tied to reality.
- **Is the language game concept fair to founders of religions?** Wittgenstein says that the meaning of language is shaped by a 'form of life' However, religious founders (Buddha, Jesus, Moses, Muhammad, Nanak, etc.) claim to have had unique experiences outside of their community. Indeed, their experiences have led to changes in the meaning of language for communities. John Hick says that if religious language only tells us about a religious form of life rather than the actual structure of reality, then religious founders have made a **mistake**. For some religions this would mean that the term 'God' may have coherence within communities but may **not correspond** to any truth outside of that community. – the same would be true for terms such as 'nirvana', 'the Law', 'karma', etc.
- **Are Wittgenstein's views self-defeating?** Some have noted that it is self-contradictory to claim that the meaning of all language is found in forms of life. This assumes that Wittgenstein is **standing outside** all forms of life in order to make this statement. In other words, if it is true that the meaning of language is found only inside a form of life, how would we ever know that this 'truth' is true for all forms of life?

Communities decide on rules – that includes the rules of language, and the meaning given to words and phrases.

❝TRIGGER QUOTES❞

All philosophy is a 'critique of language'. **(L. Wittgenstein)**

... the meaning of a word is its use in the language. **(L. Wittgenstein)**

Don't ask for the meaning, ask for the use. **(L. Wittgenstein)**

... the term 'language-game' is meant to bring into prominence the fact that the speaking of language is part of an activity, or of a form of life. **(L. Wittgenstein)**

... if you look at them [games] you will not see something that is common to all, but similarities, relationships, and a whole series of them at that. **(L. Wittgenstein)**

Specification Link

Challenges, including rejection of any true propositions in religion that can be empirically verified; does not allow for meaningful conversations between different groups of language users; does not provide adequate meaning for the word 'God'.

Quick Revision

Choose a form of life in which you have been involved (this might be a sport, an artistic endeavour, a certain club). Make a list of terms that this group uses which would be difficult to comprehend if one were not in the group. Now, write a paragraph, using AO1 Triggers in which you describe the level of difficulty one would have as a new member of this group. This will help you with an exam question on 'language games'.

❝TRIGGER QUOTES❞

In this new interpretation, religious expressions are systematically deprived of the cosmic implication that they have always been assumed to have. **(J. Hick)**

... the experience of absolute safety has been described by saying that we feel safe in the hands of God. **(L. Wittgenstein)**

❝ TRIGGER QUOTE ❞

The game that Wittgenstein was playing [was] to protect those things that he regarded as important: ethics and religion ...   **(A. C. Grayling)**

According to language games, there are barriers in our attempts at communication. For, we cannot understand the language of others without knowing the rules and practices behind their language.

Issue:

The extent to which language games provide a suitable way of resolving problems of religious language

Three evaluative controversies!

☐ **Controversy 1:** *A language games approach puts up more barriers to understanding than it removes.*

If we can only understand the meaning of another's language through a **commitment** to knowing the practices and rules which have given rise to that language, then dialogue between religious traditions (and dialogue between religionists and non-religionists) is difficult or **impossible**. It is much more effective to have a form of discourse (such as 'fact stating') through which other forms are judged. On the other hand, Wittgenstein never said that understanding was impossible between different forms of life. He only implied that one would have to **work very hard** at it.

☐ **Controversy 2:** *Language games is respectful of religious adherents.*

Solutions to the problem of religious language proposed by verificationists and falsificationists only resolve the issues if one is willing to judge religious belief by **empirical standards**. However, two sides of a dispute cannot resolve their differences without **mutual respect**. Language games provides a vehicle to find that respect by viewing both fact-stating language and various forms of religious language as **forms of life** which have their own internal coherence even if one does not understand the rules and practices that have given rise to a particular game.

☐ **Controversy 3:** *Language games does not resolve things for many religious believers!*

The language games approach is a sophisticated recognition of the power of a community to create forms of communication with **internal coherence**. Yet the focus of this approach is on the fact that language can have meaning within a community – not on the relationship of that language to **objective reality**. This leaves many religious believers uneasy. For, it implies that truth is relative and that one's religion is not true in any ultimate sense. These believers can be seen as wanting to view their creeds, scriptures and doctrines as '**fact stating**'.

Sp💡tlight: Evaluative judgements

This section contains a special insight that you can use to form a judgement.

Wittgenstein was concerned that culture would only turn to science to find meaning. His views are expressed well in this quotation: 'People nowadays think that scientists exist to instruct them; poets, musicians, etc., to give them pleasure. The idea that these have something to teach them – that does not occur to them.' Indeed, a focus on science can be blind to many sources of meaning. As is commonly said, science is sometimes guilty of 'seeing nothing in the oyster but the disease of the pearl'.

Issue:

Whether the strengths of language games outweigh the weaknesses

- **Controversy 1:** *Strength: language games challenges the* privileged position *of 'fact-stating' language.*

  The solution of logical positivists such as Ayer to the problem of religious language is to simply discount it as a source of meaning. This would leave, then, only 'fact-stating' language as a source of knowledge and guidance in life. Wittgenstein recognised that this would lead to a society which only turned to **science** to find meaning. What about art? Literature? Music? **Poetry**? Religion? Would we not be impoverished were we to see these as '**non-sense**'? Language games recognises that the empirical quest is but one form of life. Instead of dividing language into meaningful vs. non-meaningful, it compels one to see that there is language for which one knows the rules and language for which one does not yet know the rules.

- **Controversy 2:** *Weakness: it's self-defeating!*

  It is contradictory to assert that the meaning of language is found in its use with particular forms of life. This is because this assertion is intended as a **universal statement**, a level of knowledge ruled out by language games. Has Wittgenstein fallen into the same **trap** as the logical positivists – forcing a view of language onto all forms? In Wittgenstein's defense, it could be argued that he reached this view inductively through the observation of many forms of life and presents it as a '**provisional**' rather than 'final' truth for us to consider lest we fall under the spell of the logical positivists.

- **Controversy 3:** *Strength: language games has* revolutionised *epistemology.*

  Epistemology means, simply, the study of knowledge. Prior to Wittgenstein, a widely held assumption in Western philosophy was that knowledge begins when an **individual** has an experience with one of the five senses. Wittgenstein challenged this by observing how **communities** provide us with meaning and language. One does not even know the phrase 'I hurt' until this is taught – along with rules on how and when to express these words. Thus, the strength of language games is that it shows that philosophy cannot exist without insights from **sociology**, anthropology and any other means that we have to understand the role of the community in forming knowledge.

TIP

Remember, your triggers are to help you transfer your knowledge and understanding in a manageable, efficient and portable manner.

⟨TRIGGER QUOTES⟩

Philosophy may in no way interfere with the actual use of language; it can in the end only describe it. For it cannot give it any foundation either. It leaves everything as it is. **(L. Wittgenstein)**

I have no sympathy for the current European civilisation and do not understand its goals … **(L. Wittgenstein)**

Sp⊙tlight: **Evaluative judgements**

This section contains a special insight that you can use to form a judgement.

A language game can be as simple as pointing to an object and pronouncing a word – our parents 'played' this with us when we were young. But this is not as simple as it seems! There are different ways of pointing – the world of gestures. Furthermore, if the word used was 'pool', then it may have been in reference to a swimming pool or the action of playing pool. We would need to know the many rules that govern the use of this word.

AO1 Trigger revision activity

A ZIP

Language games

family resemblance	scientific inquiry	language games	respectful silence
logical positivists	monopoly	fact stating	Darth Vader
misunderstanding	analogy	rules	knowledge is formed publicly
roles	community consensus	religious practice	
practices	coherence	eternal damnation	
		quality of life	

1 Find the unhelpful Triggers! **This zip file contains several inappropriate or irrelevant Triggers**. Find these and replace them with the real Triggers from the AO1 section.

2 There's another problem: the Triggers are out of order! Put them in the same order as they appear in the AO1 section above.

3 Practise 'downloading' your zip file of Triggers from memory. See how many you can recall on first attempt.

6 Now read through your definitions and think about ways in which you could develop these using your Trigger quotes.

5 Attempt to write one clear sentence to define each Trigger.

4 When you are confident enough, order the Triggers into a list as you may do in an examination situation.

B ZIP

Challenges to language games

Anti-realism?	Fair to founders?	Self-defeating?
relativism	mistake	standing outside
dialogue is impossible	not correspond	

1 Here is your zip file of portable Triggers.

2 Practise 'downloading' your zip file of Triggers from memory. See how many you can recall on first attempt.

3 When you are confident enough, order the Triggers into a list as you may do in an examination situation.

5 Now read through your descriptions and think about ways in which you could develop these using your Trigger quotes.

4 Attempt to write one clear sentence to define each Trigger.

AO2 Trigger revision activity

A

ZIP

Language games resolving (or not) problems of religious language

Moriarty, empirical standards, mutual respect, forms of life	Barriers, commitment, impossible, Kylo Ren	Does not resolve, Thanos, objective reality, fact-stating

1 Find the unhelpful Triggers! **This zip file contains several inappropriate or irrelevant Triggers**. Find these and replace them with the real Triggers from the AO2 section.

2 There's another problem: the Triggers are out of order! Put them in the same order as they appear in the AO2 section above.

3 Practise 'downloading' your zip file of Triggers from memory. See how many you can recall on first attempt.

6 Now read through all your sentences and think about ways in which you could develop these using your Trigger quotes, further examples, and noting strengths and weaknesses.

5 Attempt to write one clear sentence to define each Trigger.

4 When you are confident enough, order the Triggers into a list as you may do in an examination situation.

B

ZIP

The strengths and weaknesses of language games

Privileged position, science, poetry, non-sense	Self-defeating! universal statement, trap, provisional	revolutionised epistemology, individual, communities, sociology

1 Here is your zip file of portable Triggers.

2 Practise 'downloading' your zip file of Triggers from memory. See how many you can recall on first attempt.

3 When you are confident enough, order the Triggers into a list as you may do in an examination situation.

5 Now read through all your sentences and think about ways in which you could develop these using your Trigger quotes, further examples, and noting strengths and weaknesses.

4 'Double-click' each Trigger in your memory – what can you say about an evaluative point of view in a clear sentence? Write this down. Do this for each Trigger in turn.

TIP

When you use a Trigger quote in an exam response, make sure that you include an explanation on how it is relevant to the question.

Using Triggers to create exam answers

Below you will find answers for sample AO1 and AO2 questions in each theme. The Triggers have been highlighted so that you can see how these have been used to form an answer to a possible exam question.

> Comments in the margins of these pages will give you added insights on qualities of an effective answer.

T2DEF: Some areas for examination

AO1

An answer using the Triggers to assist in explaining the criticisms of religion by New Atheism.

> A good introductory paragraph that highlights the main thrust of New Atheism – that religion is dangerous and harmful and needs to be stopped.

On 11 September 2001 there was a terrorist attack on the Twin Towers in New York by Islamic extremists. It was this event that was one of the main triggers for the rise of New Atheism. Atheism had regarded religion as deluded but the increasing terrorist attacks in the name of religion fuelled a view that religion wasn't just deluded, it was also dangerous and harmful to society. This more aggressive attack on religion was a hallmark of New Atheism.

The four main activists who took on this task of ridding society of religion became known as the Four Horseman. In the UK, Richard Dawkins became the best known of the four. Using various media outlets Dawkins attacked religion on a number of grounds. He forcibly argued that faith and religion are irrational and religious people are non-thinking. He claimed that 'faith is the great cop-out, the great excuse to evade the need to think and evaluate evidence'. Dawkins accused adults of forcing belief in God upon children and bringing them up to believe unquestioningly. The non-thinking went beyond sloppy thinking, it was dangerous as it led to fanaticism. It provided the climate of faith in which extremism naturally flourishes.

> A Trigger quote has been used to strengthen the response.

> Each paragraph has focused and developed on a particular criticism of religion.

New Atheism put great store on science. It rejected the choice between God or chaos as views of the universe and saw explanation in terms of natural selection rather than a God of the gaps. Indeed, religious fundamentalism subverted science since it impeded scientific progress by running away from evidence. Dawkins claimed religion sapped the intellect because it taught people not to change their mind – people were to believe without question. Dawkins argued that when a science book is wrong, someone eventually discovers the mistake and it is corrected in subsequent books. However, that does not happen with sacred religious texts. In religion, unquestioning faith is seen as a virtue.

Dawkins accounted for the power of religion by relating it to two survival mechanisms – the tendency to obey elders and, secondly, the tendency to assign meaning and purpose to animals and objects. New Atheism not only rejected the **supernatural** but attacked the character of God, **depicting God** as a misogynist, homophobic, racist, megalomaniac, sadomasochist and a capricious malevolent bully.

> This response does not judge or evaluate the criticisms of religion. This is because it is an AO1 response, focused on the key prompt 'explain'.

Evaluating and utilising the associated Triggers for the specific controversy whether or not religious responses to New Atheism have been successful.

AO2

Religious responses to New Atheism have focused on claimed misrepresentations of both religion and science. New Atheists have centred on a small group of religious extremists and labelled all religious believers with the same charge. As a result, they claim religious believers are **irrational** and **non-thinking**, and this **blind belief** leads to dangerous fanaticism. However, this denies the historical **evidence** for a faith. For example, in Christianity there is a case to be answered regards the resurrection of Jesus. In Islam there is a case for Muhammad receiving the Qur'an. There is rational debate about the evidence even though both sides may disagree. It is claimed that faith is not blind but is more about acting on what you have **good reason** to believe is true. However, many who have looked at the evidence find it wanting. It assumes the existence of the supernatural and many from the Abrahamic faiths would argue that God is not a physical object so is not open to investigation by means of the senses.

> A clear first sentence mapping out the key areas of religious response.

> A clear focus on religious responses to misrepresentations of religion and religious belief.

> Good evaluation showing reflection on the strength and persuasiveness of the previous argument.

Dawkins dismisses the arguments for God's existence in his book 'The God Delusion'. However, the religious response is that the arguments for God's existence were never claimed to be proofs but were to demonstrate the coherence of faith. Recent defences of the traditional arguments by philosophers such as Craig and Swinburne, attempt to show the arguments as justifiable rather than proven. Alister McGrath has commented that the cosmology of the 21st century is much more sympathetic to Christian belief than a century ago.

> This is a good link into the area of science in the next paragraph.

In contrast to McGrath's comment, New Atheism portrays science as the **ultimate source** of explaining everything – the definitive answer to all questions. Religions are seen as promoting ignorance and **running away** from evidence. In contrast, science gives clear answers from evidence that automatically leads to only one conclusion. It is true that there are a variety of different religious beliefs but there are also a variety of

> **A focused paragraph on a religious response to New Atheists' approach to science.**

> **Good use of Trigger quote.**

> **Some good examples of reflecting on a view.**

different conclusions based on scientific evidence. For instance, such areas as the origin of life, consciousness and multi-universes are far from agreed by the scientific fraternity. Science never gives certainties only probabilities, since the scientific method rests on falsification rather than verification. New Atheists seem to ignore the limitations of science.

Indeed, religion is seen by New Atheists as something that goes against all scientific principles. Yet it cannot be denied that there are eminent scientists who also hold a religious belief and see no conflict between the two. Professor John Lennox, a Christian and a scientist, has held many public debates with Dawkins, yet neither have been persuaded to change their views. He commented that 'the scientific explanation neither conflicts nor competes with the agent explanation'. John Polkinghorne views science and religion as offering different levels of explanation that need weaving together. However, it is true, that many scientists are not religious and see religion's world view as very different from their 'scientific' understanding. They might well claim that the religious world view includes aspects that cannot be known and so question their inclusion.

One of initial charges against religion was that religion was the root of all evil, especially regarding violence. However, religions have teachings about peace, non-violence and forgiveness as major aspects of their beliefs. But it is also true that religious beliefs have led some to acts of terrorism. The religious response has been to question whether those acts are more politically driven than religiously inspired. Also, it is argued that some have misinterpreted the true tenets of religion.

So have the religious responses been successful? It is true that New Atheism has failed to create a knockout blow to religion. If anything, New Atheism has declined. To many, it has appeared intolerant, attacking caricatures. However, because it has created debate and forced religious believers to defend their beliefs, it can be called 'successful'.

T3DEF: Some areas for examination

AO1

An answer using the Triggers to assist in explaining different definitions of 'miracle'.

> **A clear opening paragraph identifying the area and an early definition.**

The word 'miracle is derived from the Latin word for 'wonder' and its main characteristic is that it should provoke wonder, usually because it is unusual or extraordinary. However, through the centuries there have been various attempts to identify exactly what is involved in a proper conception of the miraculous. St Aquinas believed that everything that existed had a nature (i.e. the things that it is able to do). A miracle is when something takes place that is not the normal part of the nature of things.

By the 17th century, and the time of **David Hume**, the behaviour of things became expressed in terms of the **laws of nature** or natural laws, rather than in terms of their nature and the powers they had to act. Hence, he defined a miracle as 'a **transgression of a law of nature** by a particular volition of the Deity, or by the interposition of some invisible agent' – for example, the raising of a person from the dead. For Hume, miracles had to break the laws of nature and have a **divine cause**. It is a miracle regardless of whether anyone recognises it or not.

Richard Swinburne endorses Hume's view, but making **two additions**: (i) he replaces 'violation of a law of nature' with 'an occurrence of a non-repeatable counter-instance to a law of nature' (ii) he sees miracles as signs that contribute to a Divine purpose. The first addition means that the modified law is **temporary** for that one event only and the regular law of nature applies in all other circumstances. The second addition highlights the idea that miracles are done for a purpose and point to something beyond the actual event. As Swinburne has commented, 'If god intervened in the natural order to make a feather land here rather than there for no deep ultimate purpose, or to upset a child's box of toys just for spite, these events would not naturally be described as miracles.'

In contrast to Aquinas, Hume and Swinburne, **Ray Holland** advocated the idea of **contingency miracles**. He defined a miracle as 'a remarkable and **beneficial coincidence** that is interpreted in a religious way'. In his illustration of the boy in a **toy car** trapped on the railway lines, there is a **natural explanation** for why the train driver stopped the train even though he couldn't see the boy trapped on the line. The watching mother nevertheless thanked God. Holland implies that only if the **person interprets** the event as a miracle can the event be called a miracle.

> A clear focus on the second definition with good use of a quote.

> Good use of a Trigger quote.

> This answer is derived from all the Triggers given in the AO1 section in this book on the definition of miracles. This response does not judge or evaluate the definitions of miracles. This is because it is an AO1 response, focused on the key prompt 'explain'.

AO2

Evaluating and utilising the associated Triggers for the specific controversy whether or not the different definitions of miracles can be considered as contradictory.

Certainly there are differences between the various definitions of miracle. Aquinas believed that everything that existed had a nature (i.e. the things that it is able to do). So he defined a miracle as something that takes place that is not the normal part of the **nature of things**. The focus was on how the event took place. Centuries later when Hume defined a miracle, he no longer thought in terms of everything having a nature, but in terms of laws of nature – a mechanistic universe. Hume referred to a transgression of a law of nature and linked the cause to an **intervention** by a Deity or supernatural agent. However, is this a **contradiction**? It could be argued that it is merely a better understanding of our world and Aquinas implied there was a 'divine cause' since miracles were not a normal part of the nature of things. God does something that nature could not do. Both Hume and Aquinas have the notion of a divine agent.

> A clear focus on the topic.

Swinburne develops the same ideas but prefers the phrase 'an occurrence of a non-repeatable counter-instance to a law of nature'. He also refers to a divine agent but adds the idea of divine purpose. Again these are not contradictory to either Aquinas or Hume – merely clarifications and additions. However, it is with Holland's definition that perhaps some might see a contradiction. For Holland, miracles are **subjective** events – the identifying of a miracle resting solely on the decision of the individual, usually from within the circle of believers. For Swinburne, they are **objective** events –the event is miraculous, and is identified as such by both sceptic and believer. However, some may argue that this is not a contradiction as they can be **reconciled**. The different definitions are seen as describing different types of miracles. Holland's definition refers to 'contingency' miracles. Norman Geisler refers to such miracles as 'class two miracles'. A believer, possibly because of **prayer**, might see in the events a divine agency acting – and so describe it as a miracle. The type of event involving violations of laws of nature, are when the divine agency is working at a **different level**. Therefore, perhaps the definitions are merely focusing on **different aspects** and acknowledge two different types of events that can be classed as miracles (contingency and violation). On the other hand, **sceptics** would see that both subjective and objective elements in a definition help believers and their religions evade criticism – they can always 'retreat' to the contingency level if there is a lack of evidence.

Another area that may be seen as a contradiction is the very idea of the laws of nature being violated. Alistair McKinnon argued that laws of nature do not exert any opposition of resistance to anything. They have **no power** of themselves. They are simply highly generalised shorthand descriptions of how things do in fact happen. In other words, they are the **actual course of events** – the things that we observe. Therefore, to say that they are violated seems inappropriate language. It is rather than the actual course of events on that occasion, is not what we expected. However, if the laws limit what is **possible in reality** then they cannot be broken. Alternatively, if one sees the laws applying to a particular set of circumstances, then the addition of God **changes the circumstances**, such that the law no longer applies because they are now different circumstances. On this understanding – miracles do not violate the laws of nature.

In conclusion, it is true that there are different definitions, but these do not need to be considered contradictory because none of them destroy the meaning, purpose or integrity of religious experience. Whether or not a miracle violates a law of nature or works within nature, the significance of the event for the religious believer is what really matters.

Some clear reflection on the various views, showing evaluative skills. Also good use of technical language.

Another paragraph that focuses on a particular possible contradiction, with an appropriate conclusion at the end.

T4ABC: **Some areas for examination**

An answer using the Triggers to assist in explaining logical positivism.

AO1

Logical positivism refers to the position that one can have certain (or 'positive') knowledge of the world through sense perception. This knowledge can be shared and understood when it is conveyed through rational (or logical) means. Statements which may not be about the world of sense perception but conform to logical conditions such as mathematical statements and tautologies (an abstract statement that is true because of formal logical structure) also count for knowledge.

> **Key terms have been clearly explained.**

There are two types of meaningful statements that count for positive knowledge according to logical positivists such as A. J. Ayer. These are synthetic statements and analytic statements. Synthetic statements are a posteriori (based on observation and experience) and related to the objective reality ('there is a tree on the hill'). We know that such statements are meaningful through verification. In the case of synthetic statements, these are verifiable through empirical data. Furthermore, this is no private experience; the data of the tree on the hill is accessible to all. Analytic statements are a priori statements based on theoretical deduction. The truth of these statements is determined by the meaning of the terms used (2 + 2 = 4).

> **This is a good link into the area of science in the next paragraph.**

Ayer developed logical positivism by introducing a distinction between strong verification (the truth of a proposition can be immediately established in experience) and weak verification (the truth of a proposition cannot be immediately established in experience, but it is possible that it could be verified). Weak verification allows for general laws to be determined even when we cannot investigate every case.

> **Each paragraph is focused on exactly what has been asked.**

Logical positivists declared that any statements falling outside synthetic or analytic statements were to be considered meaningless. This goes further than saying these statements are 'false'; they are not considered to be genuine questions at all. This shows that the focus of logical positivism is language, ensuring that language is precise and reflects the view that there can be a single common language for all of the sciences.

> **No judgement has been about logical positivism, as this would not be appropriate for a response to an AO1 'explain' question. There is also no conclusion; a conclusion is not required for an AO1 response.**

Statements concerning matters beyond the physical world – when they are not logically necessary formulations – are meaningless. This is because they fail the criteria for synthetic statements in that they are not available for verification through empirical means. Of course, the logical positivists had religious statements in mind. As A. J. Ayer said, '... no sentence which purports to describe the nature of a transcendent god can possess any literal significance'. This means that the language of a believer (when speaking about a transcendent realm) is to be considered meaningless and outside of the scope of science. However, it is not only

> **Note the effective use of a Trigger quote which has been accompanied with a short explanation.**

religion that deals with metaphysics. Ayer noted that statements of aesthetics and morality are also meaningless.

AO2

Evaluating and utilising the associated Triggers for the specific controversy how far logical positivism should be accepted as providing a criterion for meaning in the use of language.

> **An introduction is not needed for an AO2 response. However, this brief introduction effectively sets the direction and indicates the ground that will be covered.**

This paper argues that logical positivism fails as a criterion for meaning in our use of language. It does this by considering the narrow scope of its application, modifications that have weakened the theory as well as the contradiction built into the foundation of the theory itself.

Logical positivists wanted to ensure that our use of language supported the goals of science. To this end they created a kind of **'clearing house'** for all statements. There were three rooms in this clearing house: (i) a room for analytic propositions (a priori statements, true by definition); (ii) a room for synthetic statements (a posteriori propositions, established by observation) and (iii) a very large 'bin' for meaningless statements of 'non-sense'. They argued that without such a clearing house, scientific and rational progress would be held back. However, Paul Tillich argued that this clearing house is **too small** to contain the scope of human development: '... this clearing house is a very small room, perhaps only a corner of a house, and not a real house'. Tillich meant that there are so many forms of language other than science-supporting language which humans have found meaningful. For instance, fiction, poetry, art and imagination have long taught and inspired humanity, shaping **values**, attitudes and actions. It does seem that life would be robbed of meaning if the only meaningful statements we could make were those of the logical positivists. For, we all invest meaning in the languages of love, emotions and promise-keeping in our daily lives.

> **Effective use of a Trigger quote along with an explanation.**

> **This paragraph ends with a 'mini-conclusion'; this demonstrates evaluative ability.**

Furthermore, logical positivism isn't as robust a theory as at first appears. Even Ayer himself noted that insisting on directly observable experience for every synthetic proposition was problematic For, this would mean that one could not make any claim about a past event or any scientific law. For instance, there is no direct sense experience that one can have of a past battle. Also, one cannot have an experience of every instance of gravity (i.e. strictly speaking, one may not know if an object won't drop to the ground in the future). This led to Ayer's introduction of a **'weak form'** of verification – statements can be supported by general observations about sense data. However, this has **opened the door** to faith eventually yielding verification (Basil Mitchell) and John Hick's view that a proposition can be 'eschatologically verified'. This development not only shows the original strong form of verification by the logical positivists to have been **deficient** but also points to the fact that religious faith can be seen to fit into a weak-verification approach.

> **This answer effectively refers to the 'controversies' covered in the Evaluation section.**

There is a fatal flaw in the approach of the logical positivists. The principle of verification, namely, that all meaningful propositions are either those that are logically necessary (if analytic) or empirically verifiable (if synthetic), is itself an **unverifiable** assertion. This means that it fails as a synthetic statement since it cannot be proven to be true by observation. Furthermore, if it is a tautology (a statement true by definition), then it is a purely **arbitrary** viewpoint. In either case, it would be foolish to grant authority to logical positivism as a path to determine the meaning of language since it is **self-defeating**.

> **Specialist language has been used throughout the response.**

> **A linking term has been used in order to extend a line of reasoning. This is evidence that the student has a robust understanding of the subject.**

Of course, it could be argued that despite these weaknesses, when the principles of logical positivism have been employed, science has advanced, and superstition has receded. Ayer was right to point out that much in religion, psychotherapy and morality is pseudo-science. That is, supposed statements of 'fact' may merely be assertions of prejudice, faith and emotion.

> **An opposing viewpoint has been drawn out. This is a feature of an evaluative response.**

However, it seems that dividing all language into three rooms (logically necessary, synthetic statements and non-sense') is not necessary for science to advance. There are many scientists who are able to widen the boundaries of knowledge but still find religion, poetry, fiction (etc.) sources of meaning in their lives. For instance, if a scientist says at her wedding, 'I thee wed', this language is 'non-sense' according to logical positivist standards. However, such a declaration may bring the scientist meaning in their life so as to make scientific commitments possible. It is for this reason that all knowledge **cannot be reduced** to scientific and logical formulations.

> **A clear conclusion flows from points made earlier.**

T4DEF: Some areas for examination

An answer using the Triggers to assist in explaining symbols and their function in religious language.

AO1

Paul Tillich said that symbols **participate** in a reality beyond themselves. This can be illustrated by considering a nation's **flag**. On the one hand, a flag is nothing more than a piece of fabric with various shapes and colours. However, if this was all that a flag was, this would not explain the many rules and guidelines nations have for their flags. A flag participates in something beyond itself – in this case, ideas and attitudes about one's nation. Symbols also **open up** levels of reality in our soul. That is, we are able to see and appreciate qualities of life by using symbolic language. Tillich believed that religious believers use language permeated with symbolic meaning as a way to participate in a reality beyond themselves, a metaphysical reality.

> **A key point has been supported by an example.**

For Tillich, religious symbols are symbols of the transcendent, or that which is **holy**, the ultimate ground of our being. However, the transcendent **is always beyond** the symbol; it can never be 'captured' by the symbol. **Idolatry** is the condition of viewing the symbol as holy in itself. Idolatry loses the sense that the symbol is there to point beyond itself to a greater reality.

John Randall accepted Tillich's views on symbols as pointing beyond themselves and opening up levels of reality. However, Randall was a **non-realist**, which means that he did not see 'God' as an objective reality, but as a **human creation**. He was therefore interested in how symbols function in human life. Symbols **communicate knowledge**, but this is not the same knowledge as the empirical sciences. As a creation of humans, they express human attitudes and emotions. In fact, as one studies works of art to understand the history of art, one can study symbols to understand the history of religion.

Randall said that when one studies the use of religious symbols in human history, one will see that they have four functions: (i) They **arouse** emotion and stir to action. Symbols strengthen people's commitment to what they feel is right. (ii) They **bind** a community together. A group of people may view a symbol together and thereby deepen their bond to one another. (iii) They **communicate** qualities of experience. Just as art opens up pathways of communication not available through mathematics, religious symbols open up ways to communicate. (iv) They foster and **clarify** our human experience. Religious symbols provide a pathway for people to express an 'order of splendour' they experience.

> Scholars mentioned in this part of the specification have been used.

> Knowing how scholars' views differ from one other is one sign of explanatory ability.

> One does not need to include quotations to achieve the highest mark. For, it is clear that this response knows the material in depth.

> There is no need for a conclusion; every paragraph has responded directly to the question.

AO2

Utilising the associated Triggers to evaluate how well the views of Randall and Tillich challenge logical positivism.

Logical positivists seek to restrict the amount of language that could be considered meaningful. In contrast to this, Randall and Tillich sought to enlarge this amount through examining human attitudes, feelings and emotions as expressed through symbols. This is an attractive approach because all human beings express themselves in these areas and consider their assertions to hold **meaning**. Yet, logical positivists would argue that there is a good reason why their 'room' for meaningful language is so small: aeons of energetic pursuit of symbolic meaning has led to fruitless discussions which have kept humanity trapped in **superstition**. Progress should be measured by the amount of language we devote to **analytic or synthetic** statements; all other language should be accorded a lower status. In favour of logical positivism is the fact that symbols have been bound up in outmoded beliefs. For example, a model of the solar system with the earth at the centre is just one of many symbols championed by religion against scientific discovery.

> An introduction is not essential. This response jumps right into the issues and shows evaluative depth by exploring different sides of a single issue.

> A 'mini-conclusion' has been reached on this issue. This is evidence of evaluative ability.

The discussion of symbols by Tillich and Randall is largely positive. Randall compares the study of religious symbols to the study of art history, and Tillich focuses on how symbols help us access a deeper layer of life, which he calls 'ultimate concern' and relates to the transcendent realm. However, are not symbols of **ambiguous value** for humans? It is difficult to deny Randall's point that symbols unite human communities and stir people to action. One need look no further than at a **flag** held up a the front of a charging army! Yet all of Tillich's lofty language about symbols opening up layers of meaning must be counterbalanced by the fact that symbols have been used to unleash hatred, violence and horror – one need look no further than the **swastika.** Clifford Geertz says, 'A religion is a system of symbols which acts to establish powerful, pervasive, and long-lasting moods ....' Perhaps Geertz is correct – but those 'moods' may have a negative effect and be holding humanity back from progress. It seems, then, that the logical positivists are correct to say that we should forsake the exploration of the meaning of symbols for the exploration of the world of the **senses**.

> Examples have been used to support key points.

> Note the effective use of a Trigger quote along with an explanation.

> Another 'mini-conclusion' has been reached.

Yet, it is undeniable that symbols are found in every place that humans gather. Perhaps Randall is right to suggest that **symbols are necessary** to express ourselves fully. Randall's point is that they can express a dimension of human experience that the hard sciences cannot address. Randall calls this an **'order of splendour'**, the ability to have a vision of perfection and the possibilities of human life. By rejecting this 'order of splendour' as meaningful, could logical positivists be denying what most deeply **drives human experience**? Yet, logical positivism only rejects language that does not make logical sense or cannot be verifiable. If a symbol can make sense within an analytic statement or can be verified to have meaning in a synthetic statement, then this language would transform into **cognitive language**. If not, it would be deemed meaningless. This position is applied not only to religious language but to statements of aesthetics and morality as well. In fact, it has given rise to the ethical theory of emotivism in which ethical statements are seen as mere statements of sentiment rather than having an objective basis – the same as religious language. Logical positivism seeks to 'clear the decks' of all meaningless language masquerading as certain knowledge.

> This paragraph makes use of a synoptic link to ethics in order to strengthen its argument.

In conclusion, Randall and Tillich are unable to challenge logical positivism. This is not only because, against Tillich, there is no proof of a Transcendent realm which would give religious symbolic language meaning, but because both Randall and Tillich promote symbolic religious language in a way that is blind to the pain, suffering, and ignorance it has brought into the world. When we embrace logical positivism, we may have less to speak about, but what we do say will be a solid basis for relating to the world around us.

> This paragraph reaches a reasoned conclusion which effectively uses points made earlier in the response.

Synoptic links

The table below contains suggestions for *some* synoptic links that can be made in relation to specific issues for Year 2 Philosophy. Remember (i) that using synoptic links is not a 'tick-box' exercise; only use a link if it is directly relevant to the point you are trying to explain in an AO1 response or an argument you are making in an AO2 response. (ii) The table below is not exhaustive; candidates may find more links than are listed here.

Theme/subtheme/description	Possible synoptic links
2.D. Religious belief as a product of the human mind – Sigmund Freud. Religion as an Illusion, neurosis, Oedipus complex, wish fulfilment; issues relating to adequacy of explanation.	• God as Father/Mother figure (Christianity YR1) • Feminist theology (Christianity YR2) • Celebration of the Eucharist (Christianity YR1) • Theories of Atonement (Christianity YR1) • The roles of men and women in the various religious traditions (e.g. Buddhism YR2, Hinduism YR 2) • Divine Command Theory (Ethics YR1) • Natural Law (Ethics YR1)
2.E. Religious belief as a product of the human mind – Carl Jung. Religion necessary for personal growth; individuation, archetypes; issues relating to Jung more positive than Freud and Jung's empirical approaches.	• The nature of God (Christianity YR 1) • Religious experience e.g. mystical and Otto and the numinous (Philosophy YR1) • Various religious beliefs about the meaning and purpose of life (e.g. Judaism YR1) • Virtue ethics (Ethics YR1)
2.F. Rejection of religion – Atheism. Differences between agnosticism and atheism, the rise of New Atheism, its main criticisms of religion and religious responses; issues relating to the success of the arguments.	• Historical questioning of birth and resurrection (Christianity YR1) • The nature of God (Christianity YR 1) • Failure of arguments for God (Philosophy YR1) • Problem of evil (Philosophy YR1) • Challenges to religious experience (Philosophy YR1) • Views of Jesus (Christianity YR2) • Various religious traditions challenges from secularisation and science (e.g. Hinduism YR2) • Utilitarianism as a secular theory (Ethics YR1) • Religious language issues (Philosophy YR2)

Theme/subtheme/description	Possible synoptic links
3.D. Religious experience influencing religious practice and faith. Value for religious community, value for individual; issues relating to impact and dependence on religious experience.	• Examples of religious practice and ritual in the various religious traditions • Examples of religious festivals in the various religious traditions • Religious experiences of founders and religious figures • Challenges to religious experience (Philosophy YR1) • Charismatic movement (Christianity YR2) • Sufi practices (Islam YR2) • Kabbalah (Judaism YR2) • Mindfulness movement (Buddhism YR2) • Samkhya yoga and Advaita Vedanta (Hinduism YR2)
3.E and 3.F. Definition and possibility of miracles. Various definitions, David Hume and his scepticism, Richard Swinburne and his defence of miracles; issues relating to adequacy and contradiction of the definitions, validity of challenge to belief.	• Miracle accounts in religious texts e.g. Jesus and the virgin birth and Jesus' resurrection (Christianity YR1) • Crossan, Bultmann and Wright (Christianity) • Charismatic movement (Christianity YR2) • God of gaps/limits of science (Christianity YR2) • Festivals based on a miraculous event • Atheism (Philosophy YR2)

Theme/subtheme/ description	Possible synoptic links
4.A. Problems of religious language **4.B. Religious language: cognitive but meaningless**	**Component 1 – The Study of Religion** The subthemes of religious language are overlapping, raising issues having to do with the truth and/or value of literalism, symbolism and myth in religions. Students can feel free to link these themes to issues in the religion they are studying. Of particular relevance are: • Accounts of creation – are these taken literally or mythologically? • The significance of 'events' in the lives of founders to the religion – are these viewed as historical or mythological?
4.C. Non-cognitive and analogical **4.D. Non-cognitive and symbolic** **4.E. Non-cognitive and mythological** **4.F. Religious language as a language game**	**Christianity:** • Bultmann's mythological views in YR1 (1B) and YR2 (1E) • Wright's critical realism in YR2 (1F) • Sallie McFague's views on metaphors vs. literalistic language. YR1 (2A) • Dawkins' critique of literalistic religious claims in 3F • The McGraths' idea of POMA (partially overlapping magisterial) YR2 (3E) • Hick's views on religious language YR2 (3F) • Augustine and Zwingli on symbols YR1 (4A) • Transignification and transfinalisation as symbolic approaches vs. the literal understanding of transubstantiation YR1 (4B) • Verification of charismatic experiences YR2 (4E) **Islam** • The concept of revelation as literal words from God/Islamic views of translations YR1 (1A and 1C) • Attributes of God as metaphors and symbols YR 1 (2A) • Depictions of Heaven and Hell YR1 (2C) • Teachings on creation and their compatibility with modern scientific theories YR2 (3B) • Modernist approaches to crime and punishment YR2 (4F) **Judaism** • The roles of Torah in orthodox vs. reform Judaism YR1 (1C) • Contrasting views on the Messiah |The Pittsburgh platform and reform views about the afterlife YR1 (2C) • Various interpretations of the Mitzvot YR1 2D • The challenge of science, creation and evolution YR2 (3B) • Views of reform and orthodox to interfaith dialogue YR2 (3C) • Symbols in Kabbalah YR2 (4E) **Component 3 – Ethics** The following topics could be relevant to specific issues of religious language • Divine command theory and objective truth YR1 (1A) • Virtue ethics and cultural relativism YR1 (1B) • Naturalism and objective moral laws YR2 (1D) • Objective moral laws and intuitionism YR2 (1E) • Emotivism as a non-cognitivist theory YR2 (1F) • Natural Law approaches (in both YR1 and YR2) as basing themselves on objective reality

- Sources of authority – as interpreted literally or analogically/symbolically.
- Challenges of science to literalistic and modernist interpretations.
- The coherence of the philosophy or doctrines in a particular religion (or religious tradition) as a language-game.

Specific content that students may draw from:

Buddhism
- The birth narratives – mythological interpretations YR1 (1A)
- The importance of the Pali canon YR2 (1D)
- No speculation on metaphysical questions YR1 (2B)
- The Four noble truths as accurate accounts of reality YR1 (2D)
- Challenges to Buddhism from science YR2 (3B)
- Buddhism as a rational philosophy YR2 (3C)
- Buddhism as true to experience YR2 (3D)
- Philosophical understandings of the nature of reality YR2 (4E)

Hinduism
- The relevance of Hindu texts to the modern world YR1 (1A, 1B)
- The relationship between atman-brahman as a language game? (YR1 2A | YR2 1D)
- Trimurti and related concepts as mythological/analogical? YR1 (2B)
- Mythical origins of the Varnashramadharma YR1 (2D)
- The relationship between Hinduism, secularism and science YR2 (3B)
- The stories behind religious practices as literal or mythological (noting the role of symbols) YR1 (4ABC)
- Philosophical understandings of the nature of reality YR2 (4E)

Sikhism
- 5Ks [as having literal or symbolic meaning] YR1 (1B)
- The status of the GGS YR1 (1C)
- Understandings of 'God' and 'the soul' YR1 (2A; 2B)
- Concepts such as karma and sewa [interpreted literally?] YR1 (2C) and YR2 (2D)
- Relationship of feminism with Sikh religious philosophy YR2 (3B)
- Challenges to Sikhism from science and secularism YR2 (3D)
- The meaning given to the stories represented in festivals YR1 (4ABC)
- Evidence of a personal mystical union with God YR2 (4E)
- The meaning of names for God YR2 (4E)

- Situation ethics and moral relativism YR1 (3ABC)
- Utilitarianism as a 'scientific' approach YR1 (3DEF)
- Predestination and religious free will could be examined as each internally coherent, as language games YR2 (4A, 4D)
- Sartre's existentialism as non-cognitive and relativist YR2 (4E)

AO1 responses: essential guidance

These insights will help you to meet the WJEC/Eduqas criteria for knowledge and understanding in an examination setting.

1. Make sure your first sentence responds directly to the question.
You will then maintain this same focus throughout your answer. For example, if you are responding to a question which asks you to explain Hume's challenges to the credibility of witnesses of miracles (3F), your first sentence might be 'Hume gave three reasons why the quality of the testimony required to establish the occurrence of a miracle can never be forthcoming.'

2. You do not need an introduction or conclusion for an AO1 question.
Having an introduction or conclusion may mean that you end up repeating information or including material that is not relevant – this material will not gain you any extra marks. For example, if you are asked to explain Swinburne's definition of a miracle, you may be tempted to discuss the other definitions as a general introduction to the definition of miracles. However, doing this is not a response to the question. Rather, you should begin by directly discussing the key elements of Swinburne's definition.

3. Know how to use quotations correctly.
A relevant quote can strengthen an explanation in an AO1 response – that's why 'Trigger quotes' have been included in this guide. Always include an explanation of the quotation and why it is important for the explanation you are making. For instance, in a response that examines the religious responses to New Atheism (2F) you could include a Trigger quote from John Lennox (just under the AO1 Triggers for that section). But don't let the quote do the work for you – write a sentence remarking on the meaning of the quote or how it relates to the question that has been asked.

4. Use scholars, examples and sources as often as possible to explain key points.

For example in section 3E, where Aquinas, Hume, Swinburne and Holland are named in relation to miracles, you will want to ensure you can speak about each scholar in depth; if they have used examples, illustrations or key ideas (such as Holland's example of the boy in the toy car caught on the rail tracks or Swinburne and his non-repeatable counter-instance) you can explore these in order to show that you grasp their viewpoints in depth.

5. Include specialist language in your answer.

This is a sign that you have studied an area with depth. However, you will not be awarded any marks for 'dropping terms' into an answer when it is clear that you do not know the meaning of the words you are using. For instance, if you were using terms such as archetypes or individuation (2E) to describe Jung's views, you would want to make sure you indicated you knew the terms by discussing how Jung sees religion as necessary for personal growth.

6. Wandering into biographical details or related subjects – when this is not asked for by the question – will hold you back.

If, for example, you are asked to explain the meaning of the Oedipus complex (2D) and include a discussion of the birthplace and religious upbringing of Freud, this will not gain you any marks – even if the information you have shared is accurate. Always remain focused on the question.

7. For Year 2 Students: include a synoptic link, but only where appropriate.

This means including an idea from one of the other two areas of the course. For instance, if you are asked to examine challenges to religious experience, you may want to bring in some of the challenges from science to the religion you have studied when these criticism claims for religious experience. How many links do you need in a paper? There is no magic number. Indeed, trying to force a link that doesn't quite 'fit' or use a formula will weaken your paper; you would be better off not attempting a synoptic link. However, a single, well-placed link in an answer will be fulfilling the highest band: 'insightful connections are made between the various approaches studied'.

AO2 responses: essential guidance

These insights will help you to meet the WJEC/Eduqas criteria for evaluation in an examination setting.

1. Delve into evaluative issues, engaging with the material you present.
The heart of your paper is your examination of controversies relevant to the question, with attention to scholars and/or sources of wisdom. This is why three controversies have been outlined for you with every issue. For example, if you need to make an evaluative response to the issue of religious language as meaningful vs. meaningless religious language, you can be guided by the three controversies that are outlined for this area in the AO2 section for Theme 4B.

2. Support your evaluation with quotes, references and examples.
For example, your presentation of a controversy will be strengthened by including a relevant Trigger quote from this revision guide. Let's say you are presenting the controversy over the whether or not logical positivism provides a valid criterion for meaning in the use of language. This is the second issue from the AO2 section in 4B. You can support your evaluation by using one of the Trigger quotes underneath the controversies section such as the one from T. Maudlin. Your task would be to show how the quote speaks to this controversy.

3. Continually review and reflect on the arguments you present.
In other words, don't hold all of your conclusions until the end of the paper. For example, you can add a mini-conclusion to the discussion of a specific controversy. This is your provisional viewpoint on just one of the controversies you are covering prior to your overall conclusion at the end of the answer. Let's say that you are evaluating the validity of non-cognitive responses to the challenges of logical positivists. One issue that you might explore is that a non-cognitivist approach actually is not embraced by many religious believers. You can wrap up that part of the discussion up with a 'mini-conclusion': 'Religious believers are right to insist that there is a correspondence of their beliefs to objective reality because, otherwise, they would find it difficult to commit time and resources to their beliefs when they could embrace any number of other commitments.' This is a 'provisional conclusion'; you might even disagree with it in your final conclusion, but it shows that your 'evaluative brain' is engaged throughout your answer.

4. **A short introduction can set a great tone.**
It is not necessary to have an introduction, but a few sentences at the beginning of the paper that include specialist language and an indication of some of the relevant issues you are going to examine can help the examiner see that you are 'in the zone'. Stating a position in the introduction is optional. Some students declare a position on an issue at the beginning of their response and then 'check in' on that position as they move through their response. It is equally acceptable to not come to a position until the end of the answer.

5. **Be fair to positions that are not your own.**
One sign of strong evaluative ability is to represent positions that are not your own fairly and with depth. One way to practise doing this is to adopt a position that is not your own. For example, if you consider that religious symbols do not speak to a transcendent reality, ensure that you have represented the views of Paul Tillich who argued that they do and are therefore necessary to speak to the mysterious depth of human experience.

6. **Conclude by stating a position and justifying it.**
This position may be stated in the 'third person' ('It seems clear that ...') or in the first person ('I think that ...' or 'I believe that ...') However, what is most important is that this statement is followed by a justification for your position. You can do this by looking back at the various arguments you have presented and also at your 'mini-conclusions'. Then, restate these in a new way.

7. **For Year 2 Students: include a synoptic link, but only where appropriate.**
This means bringing an idea in from one of the other two areas of the course. For instance, if you are writing an answer on the extent to which the concept of language games resolves problems of religious language, you might find it natural to present how a specific doctrinal or philosophical approach in the religion you have studied has an internal coherence which is understood by many religious believers. How many links are needed in a response? There is no magic number. Indeed, trying to 'shoe-horn' a link that doesn't really 'fit in' will weaken your paper. However, one well-placed link in an answer will fulfill one of the requirements of the highest band: 'insightful connections are made between the various approaches studied'.

Index